First published in the UK in 2025 by Studio Press,
an imprint of Bonnier Books UK
5th Floor, HYLO, 105 Bunhill Row,
London, EC1Y 8LZ

Copyright © Rachael Taylor, 2025

1 3 5 7 9 10 8 6 4 2

All rights reserved
ISBN 978-1-83587-333-5

Written by Rachael Taylor
Edited by Stephanie Milton
Designed by Alessandro Susin
Production by Holly Porter

This book is unofficial and unauthorised and
is not endorsed by or affiliated with Omega.

A CIP catalogue record for this book
is available from the British Library

Printed and bound in China

The authorised representative in the EEA is Bonnier Books
UK (Ireland) Limited.
Registered office address: Floor 3, Block 3, Miesian Plaza,
Dublin 2, D02 Y754, Ireland
compliance@bonnierbooks.ie

www.bonnierbooks.co.uk

The publisher would like to thank the following for supplying photos for this book: Omega, Alamy, Getty and Shutterstock. Every effort has been made to obtain permission to reproduce copyright material but there may be cases where we have not been able to trace a copyright holder. The publisher will be happy to correct any omissions in future printing.

OMEGA

The Story Behind the Style

RACHAEL TAYLOR

Contents

Timekeeper of the World (and Beyond)	6
A Watchmaker with a Vision	8
Omega at War	22
Post-war Innovation	24
Swatch Group	28
Moments in History	30
First Watch on the Moon	32
The Alaska Project	36
The Snoopy Speedmasters	38
Dark Side of the Moon	40
Timing the Olympics	42
The Deepest Dive	46
Licensed to Thrill	48
Innovations	52
The First Dive Watch	54
The First Tourbillon Movement	58
An Early Swiss Quartz Movement	60
The Co-Axial Escapement	64
Anti-Magnetic Movement	66
The Icons	68
Seamaster	70
Constellation	72
Ladymatic	74
Speedmaster	76
Railmaster	78
De Ville	82
Diver 300M	84
Aqua Terra	86

Constellation Globemaster	88
Seamaster Planet Ocean	90
De Ville Trésor	92
Swiss Made	**94**
The Manufacture	96
Movements	100
Precision	102
Testing	107
Materials	108
Museum	110
Planet Omega	**112**
Olympics and Paralympics	114
Sailing	116
Swimming	118
Bobsleigh	120
Golf	122
Athletics	124
Omega on Film	**126**
The Art of Collecting	**130**
Vintage Omega	132
Speedy Tuesdays	134
Rare Omegas	136
Omegas at Auction	140
Positive Impact	**142**
Sustainability At Sea	144
GoodPlanet Foundation	146
Space Debris	148
Orbis	150
An Eco Build	152
Enduring Legacy	**154**

Timekeeper of the World (and Beyond)

Omega is a brand that resonates far beyond the rarified cloisters of watch collectors. It is a household name synonymous with precision, prestige and adventure. To slip an Omega onto your wrist is to associate yourself with a legacy that touches the electrifying highs of the Olympics, the mysterious depths of the oceans, and even otherworldly orbits.

The company's journey began in 1848, when a young watchmaker named Louis Brandt began assembling pocket watches in a small workshop in a Swiss town. What followed was a journey of innovation and ambition that would lead to Omega becoming one of the most trusted names in timekeeping.

As you will discover, Omega carved out its place in history by thinking boldly and acting precisely. It has revolutionised the world of sports timekeeping, was the first watch on the moon, and its high-profile partnerships have jettisoned its watches onto screens both big and small the world over.

Omega has always stood at the intersection of form and function by balancing style with innovative horological advancements. Its watches are worn by astronauts and actors, deep-sea divers and diplomats. They are a symbol of technical mastery, wrapped in timeless style.

And this is the story behind that style – the people, the moments, and the mechanisms that made Omega a legend.

OPPOSITE: Louis Brandt, the watchmaker who laid the foundations for the Omega brand.

ABOVE: Omega wristwatch produced for the French market, circa 1946.

A Watchmaker with a Vision

To understand the origin story of Omega, we must travel back in time to 19th-century Switzerland and the town of La Chaux-de-Fonds, nestled high in the Jura Mountains. It was here, in 1848, that a 23-year-old watchmaker named Louis Brandt set up a modest workshop. In doing so, he laid the foundation for what would become one of the world's most famous and loved watch brands.

At the time, La Chaux-de-Fonds was already a vibrant hub of horology. Its distinctive grid-like layout – the result of the town being partially rebuilt after a fire in 1794 – was designed to maximise light in the buildings. This was an architectural rarity in Switzerland and, in combination with the purpose-built roads and buildings that emerged after the fire, made it the ideal location for crafts that required a keen eye, such as watchmaking.

Brandt joined a growing number of industrious craftsmen in La Chaux-de-Fonds, and began assembling key-wound pocket watches using parts supplied by local producers. These early watches were manually wound with a key, which was the standard at that time, before the widespread adoption of the stem-winding mechanism.

OPPOSITE: An illustration of La Chaux-de-Fonds in 1848.

LEFT: An Art Deco-style women's watch made by Omega in 1920.

Brandt was passionate about precision, and within a few years the young watchmaker cultivated a reputation for delivering highly accurate timepieces. His horological renown spread, first through Switzerland and then beyond. Historical records show that Brandt would travel personally to visit clients in Italy, Scandinavia and England.

As Brandt's business grew, his sons Louis-Paul and César Brandt joined him, and the company name of Louis Brandt & Fils was registered in 1877. Brandt would pass away just two years later, but his sons carried on the family business and took it to new heights.

Despite the loss of its founder, Louis Brandt & Fils was thriving, and the brothers realised they needed more space than the workshop in La Chaux-de-Fonds could afford. So, in 1880 they made a bold move to change location, setting up 45km away in Bienne. Their first address was 119 Route de Boujean, before moving to 96 Rue Jakob-Stämpfli – which remains the address of Omega today.

Not only did this new town offer more space to grow, it also had better transport links and hydro-powered factories. It was also home to a glut of suppliers and manufacturers for Louis Brandt & Fils to source from, and a workforce that was better suited to factory-based manufacturing than the artisanal cottage industry experts they had left behind in La Chaux-de-Fonds.

OPPOSITE: The Omega factory in Biel/Bienne in 1910.

ABOVE: A view from inside Omega's factory in 1920.

As such, this move marked a crucial turning point, allowing the brothers to modernise their business. While Louis Brandt & Fils maintained the family commitment to quality, the next generation were determined to shift away from the traditional *établissage* – artisanal – system of watchmaking in which parts are sourced from different suppliers and assembled piecemeal. Instead, the Brandt brothers introduced an integrated manufacturing model, aiming to bring as many processes as possible under one roof. This allowed for greater consistency, faster production and, ultimately, more innovation.

Under this new setup Omega could produce watch movements in larger quantities by using standardised rather than individually handcrafted parts, meaning each one could be assembled more quickly and more reliably. This led to the creation of their first series-produced calibre in 1885, which they called Labrador.

The Labrador movement marked a major technological leap forward, delivering exceptional accuracy and build quality for its time. It was the company's first real step towards large-scale, standardised watchmaking. With the Labrador, Omega showed the world that precision could go hand in hand with efficient production – an ethos that would define the brand's future.

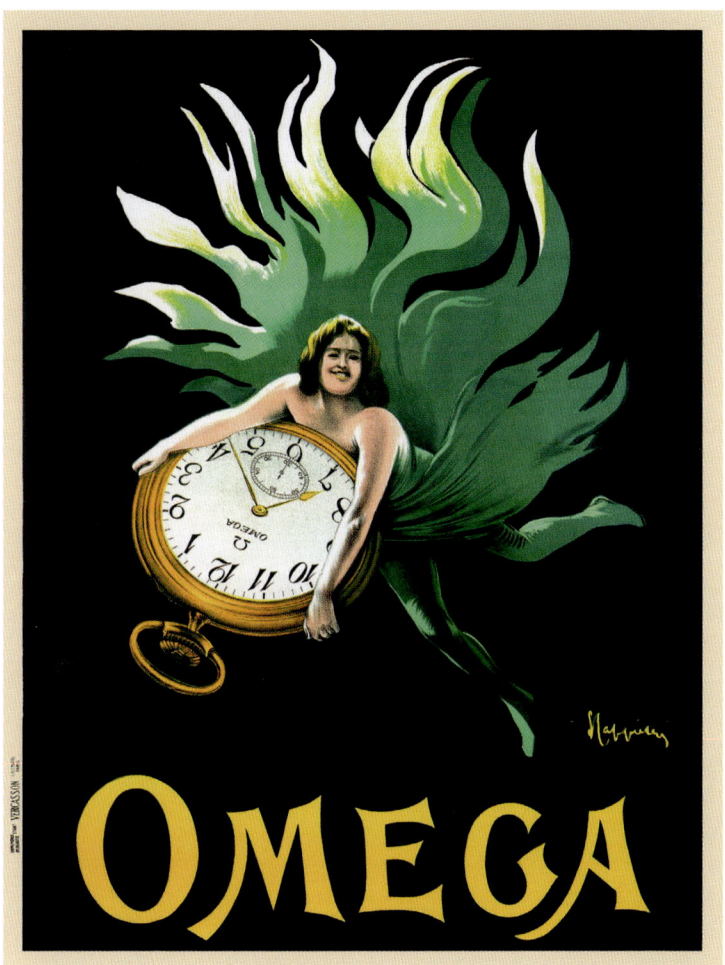

OPPOSITE: Omega watchmakers at work in Switzerland in 1920.

ABOVE: A vintage Omega advertisement illustrated by Leonetto Cappiello, circa 1910.

LEFT: An 1894 advert for Omega's 19-Ligne Calibre.

OPPOSITE: One of the first Omega chronographs, circa 1900.

More innovation followed. In 1892, the Brandt brothers collaborated with watchmaker Audemars Piguet to create what is thought to be the world's first minute-repeating wristwatch. A minute repeater is a highly complex mechanical complication that chimes the hours, quarters and minutes on demand, allowing the time to be heard as well as seen. It was a useful function for the days before widespread electric lighting, but was still charming in the late 19th century, by which time many homes had introduced this innovation.

This groundbreaking one-of-a-kind watch (only one was ever produced) is somewhat unassuming considering its landmark horological prowess. It has an unbranded white enamel dial, with a seconds sub dial, looped by an 18-karat gold case on a leather strap.

You can see it for yourself in the Omega Museum in Biel/Bienne, as the town is now known after the decision was made in 2005 to merge the German and French names for the bi-lingual city.

In 1894, Louis Brandt & Fils revealed another innovation: its 19-ligne pocket watch calibre, which would change the course of the business, and the wider watchmaking industry. The calibre was named for its size – a ligne is an old French unit used specifically in horology to measure the diameter of watch movements, with 19 ligne the equivalent to about 43 millimetres. The 19-ligne calibre was highly accurate, easy to repair, and designed with industrial-scale manufacturing in mind. For the first time, every component of the movement could be replaced without the need for custom fitting – a revolutionary idea in an era when most timepieces were still handmade.

ABOVE: A rare prototype of an automobile dashboard clock fitted with a chronograph.

The 19-ligne was so successful that the brothers gave it a name: Omega. Named after the final letter of the Greek alphabet, it symbolised perfection and completion. The name caught on so quickly, and sales of the Omega calibre were so strong that Louis Brandt & Fils rebranded that same year to Omega Watch Co, in order to capitalise on its popularity. The following year, in 1895, Omega debuted its first official brand imagery, an illustration of Chronos – the Greek god of time – atop a globe inscribed with the Omega name, and holding a pocket watch and pointing a lance to the brand name. It was a powerful symbol of Omega's global ambitions.

At a time when globalisation was still in its infancy, Omega was exporting timepieces to markets as far afield as the United States, China and South America. It was also winning critical acclaim, receiving the Grand Prize at the 1900 Universal Exposition in Paris in recognition of its advancements in horology.

It was one of the first Swiss watchmakers to operate as a true international brand, supported by a reliable production system that could deliver high volumes without compromising on quality. Retailers across the globe advertised that they were carrying the world-famous Omega watches to draw in customers. At G and T Young in Oamaru, New Zealand, in 1903 – by which time Omega was the largest manufacturer of finished watches in Switzerland – you could buy one for 26 shillings. By 1909, Omega was selling on six continents.

The business was going great guns, until the global financial crash of 1929 hit the Swiss watch industry hard. In an attempt to strengthen its position, Omega formed an alliance with fellow Swiss watch brand Tissot. In 1930, the two companies merged to form SSIH (Société Suisse pour l'Industrie Horlogère) to share resources and research.

In the early decades of the 20th century, Omega began to create a number of associations that would raise the profile of the brand. It became a supplier to the military as well as the railway. It also started to align itself with sporting events, which would prove to be a particularly savvy move. In 1932, Omega was chosen as the official timekeeper of the Olympic Games – a title it holds to this day.

Throughout this period, Omega also played a crucial role in the evolution of wristwatches. Like many early wristwatch manufacturers, it answered the early 20th century trend for watches by adapting pocket watch movements to be worn on the wrist. But soon it started designing movements and cases specifically for this smaller, more wearable format. One of Omega's most notable early wristwatches was worn by British Royal Flying Corps pilots in World War I, and had a robust design and legible dial that proved ideal for military use. For many soldiers, war was the first time they had worn a timepiece on the wrist, as it was previously deemed a woman's object. They had no pockets in which to place a pocket watch and the mandated wristwatch for men, which was much more practical than a pocket watch during the trials of war, sparked a post-war trend as men grew used to the design.

OPPOSITE: A 1932 advert for Omega watches, featuring an Olympian.

ABOVE: British World War I aviators - Omega supplied the army with trench watches.

Post-war, Omega focused on improving precision, and in 1931 its chronometers set new records in all six categories of the Geneva Observatory trials. Doing so meant the timepieces were more accurate across a range of conditions than any other watch tested at that time.

Omega would follow this with a world precision record in 1936, when an Omega calibre scored an extraordinary 97.8 out of 100 at the Kew Observatory – a result so precise it remains unbeaten to this day.

The 1930s were a period of much innovation for Omega. In 1931, it pioneered a groundbreaking automatic movement prototype that used two weights to wind the mechanism in both directions – a leap in efficiency that laid the foundation for the modern self–winding watches we know today.

Then, a year later, it launched the Marine, the world's first commercially available divers' watch. The Marine featured a patented double case sealed with cork to protect against water seeping inside, and had an adjustable clasp with a divers' extension.

This – and other innovations introduced by Omega – would prove valuable when World War II broke out across Europe at the end of the decade.

OPPOSITE: A 1951 advert in French that celebrates the Geneva Observatory trials the year before.

LEFT: A 1932 Omega Marine watch, the world's first commercially available divers' watch.

Omega at War

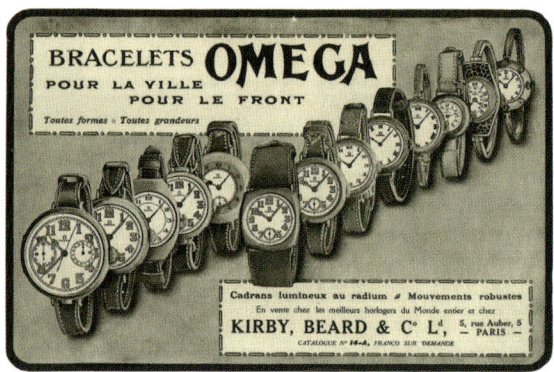

In times of war, precision can mean the difference between chaos and coordination, and Omega played its role in helping soldiers to achieve the latter in both World War I and World War II.

During World War I, Omega produced thousands of rugged trench watches. These early wristwatches were adapted from pocket watch designs and had luminous numerals to help soldiers better read the time in poor visibility, shrapnel guards and robust cases suited for the mud and mayhem of the battlefield.

By the time World War II was wreaking havoc across Europe and beyond, Omega was the British military's single largest watch contractor. In 1940, the Swiss watchmaker was commissioned to produce tens of thousands of watches for the British armed forces and its allies.

This contract prompted Omega to accelerate its advances in water resistance, shock protection and anti-magnetic performance. And these innovations were tested to their limits on the front lines.

Among Omega's standout wartime models was the CK2129 pilot's watch, also sometimes known as the Weems watch after its designer Philip van Horn Weems. The watch was issued to RAF bomber crews and equipped with a rotating bezel for timing missions, and helped airmen synchronise with radio signals mid-flight. The CK2129 featured on the big screen in 2017 as the watch worn by Tom Hardy's Spitfire pilot in the film *Dunkirk*.

Between 1939 and 1945, Omega delivered more than 110,000 watches to the Allied forces. In the crucible of global conflict, Omega watches earned a reputation for their unwavering dependability, even in the most difficult of circumstances.

OPPOSITE: A 1916 advert promoting Omega's trench watches that reads 'for the city, for the front'.

LEFT: An example of a CK2129 watch that was worn by World War II pilots.

Post-war Innovation

The post-war years marked a period of reinvention and technical progress for Omega. As the world began rebuilding after World War II, Omega channelled its wartime expertise into innovation that would shape the future of wristwatches.

In 1946, Omega released the bold and stylish Tubogas, a rare 18-karat rose gold women's dress watch designed for the French market. Italian jeweller Bulgari would become famed for the execution of this technique (which involves coiling thin interlocking

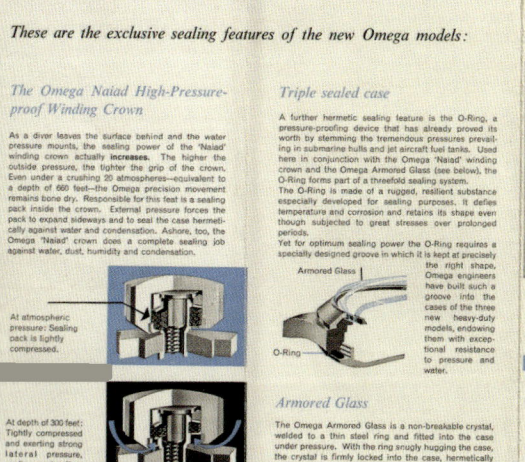

strips of gold to create a flexible structure that requires no soldering) within its Serpenti collection, but Omega pipped it by two years.

The release of the Omega Tubogas was accompanied by an advertisement illustrated by famed fashion artist René Gruau that blended haute horologerie and haute couture. Although for Omega – a watchmaker, not a jeweller – this technique proved too difficult and time consuming to produce at scale, so only a few of these watches were ever made.

A year later, in 1947, Omega pushed the limits of mechanical watchmaking by creating one of the world's first tourbillon wristwatch movements, the calibre 30I. Previously confined to pocket watches, tourbillons were prized for their ability to counteract the effects of gravity on timekeeping. Omega's miniaturised version proved that this complex mechanism – regularly employed in today's luxury watches – had a place on the wrist.

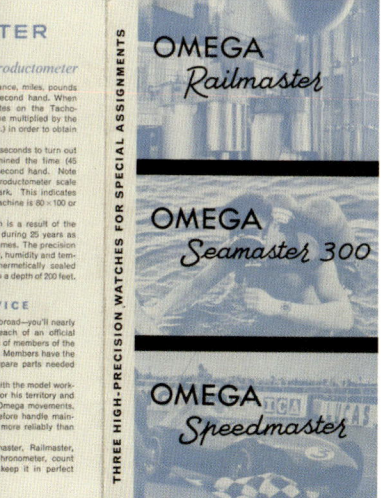

In 1948, marking the watchmaker's centenary, Omega launched the Seamaster, which would become one of the most iconic watches of all time. The Seamaster was inspired by the brand's military heritage and featured an innovative O-ring gasket system inspired by technology used in submarines. The gasket helped to improve the watch's moisture resistance.

LEFT: Marketing material for the Omega Speedmaster produced in 1957.

This spirit of progress continued in the 1950s with a string of landmark releases. In 1952, Omega unveiled the Constellation, a chronometer-certified dress watch named after the stars, and marked by an observatory medallion on its caseback.

Then, in 1957, Omega launched a trio of professional watches that would shape the future of its tool watches – the Speedmaster, the Seamaster 300, and the Railmaster.

The Speedmaster, designed for motorsports, introduced a now-iconic chronograph layout with a tachymeter on the bezel. It was the first of its kind, as the tachymeter (a scale used to measure speed based on time and distance) was printed on the bezel rather than on the dial, as was the norm.

The Seamaster 300 took diving watches to new depths quite literally, as it was water resistant to 200 metres. This might seem confusing considering the model's name – Omega did test the watch internally to 300 metres although only publicly advertised it as being suitable to depths of 200 metres. The Seamaster 300 had a rotating bezel for timing dives, and luminous visibility under water, making it a favourite among naval divers and adventurers.

Completing the trilogy was the Railmaster, a watch created for scientists, engineers and railway workers. It had a double-case construction designed to resist magnetic fields, which was a vital feature in an age when electronics and heavy machinery in certain professions posed a growing threat to mechanical precision.

Collectively, these watches defined an era, proving that Omega was not only keeping pace with the times, but setting the tempo.

OPPOSITE: A vintage Omega Constellation watch, with a view of its signature caseback.

BELOW: A vintage Omega Railmaster watch on a leather strap.

Swatch Group

By the early 1980s, the Swiss watch industry was in turmoil. The so-called Quartz Crisis, triggered by the rise of inexpensive, battery-powered watches from Asia, had upended the mechanical watch market, leaving many of Switzerland's most storied brands struggling. Omega was among them.

A route to survival presented itself in 1983, when Omega became part of a newly consolidated holding company formed by two major Swiss watch groups: Omega's parent company SSIH and ASUAG (Allgemeine Schweizerische Uhrenindustrie AG).

This union would evolve into what we now know as the Swatch Group, founded by visionary entrepreneur Nicolas G. Hayek. His mission was to save Swiss watchmaking by merging tradition with modern manufacturing and bold marketing, and Omega played a pivotal role in that revival.

Under Swatch Group leadership, Omega began to reclaim its position as a global luxury leader. The brand doubled down on its heritage, reissuing icons like the Speedmaster and Seamaster, while investing in new technologies such as Co-Axial escapements, Master Chronometer certification and anti-magnetic movements. Omega also embraced high-profile partnerships – including becoming watch brand of choice to James Bond, reinforcing its visibility and cultural relevance.

The Swatch Group not only stabilised Omega during a moment of crisis for the Swiss watch industry, it also gave the brand the scale, investment, and creative freedom to keep innovating. As such, Omega emerged from the Quartz Crisis stronger than ever, with a clear identity.

OPPOSITE: Formula 1 World Champion and Omega ambassador Michael Schumacher (center) with Swatch Group executives Nicolas Hayek and Stephen Urquhart in 2005.

ABOVE: Former Swatch Group president Nicolas Hayek pictured in Lausanne, Switzerland, in 2001.

Moments in History

Throughout its history, Omega has been present to capture the exact moment the world changed, many times over. Omega watches have accompanied astronauts on history-making missions, divers into previously uncharted depths, and athletes to record-breaking finish lines. Whether achieving what had been thought humanly impossible or taking an out-of-this world "small step for man", many pioneers whose actions have made giant leaps for mankind have done so with an Omega nearby. This has led to the Swiss brand becoming so much more than just a watchmaker. It could well be considered history's timekeeper.

ABOVE: The Ultra Deep watch strapped to the arm of a submersible in its way to the bottom of the Mariana Trench.

OPPOSITE: The Apollo 17 launch at the Kennedy Space Center in Florida in 1972. (Image courtesy of NASA).

First Watch on the Moon

On July 20, 1969, as Neil Armstrong and Buzz Aldrin become the first humans to walk on the moon during the Apollo 11 mission, Omega was earning its own place in history. The Omega Speedmaster Professional, strapped to Aldrin's spacesuit, became the first watch worn on the moon. While the trip to the moon was certainly a major marketing coup for Omega, the astronauts did actually use the watches as tools for navigation and timing.

OPPOSITE: Astronaut Buzz Aldrin wearing an Omega Moonwatch.

LEFT: The Omega Speedmaster Professional, reference 310.30.42.50.01.001.

NASA's decision to select the Omega Speedmaster was the result of intense testing. In the mid-1960s, the space agency issued a call to several watch manufacturers, seeking a timepiece that could endure the challenging conditions of space travel. The testing regimen was famously brutal: exposure to extreme heat, cold, vacuum, humidity, shock, acceleration, decompression and vibration.

The three main contenders were the Omega Speedmaster, Rolex Chronograph Ref. 6238, and Longines-Wittnauer 235T. Of all the watches submitted, only the Omega Speedmaster passed all of NASA's tests.

In 1965, the Speedmaster was officially certified by NASA, earning the designation 'Flight Qualified for All Manned Space Missions'. From that moment on, it accompanied astronauts on the Mercury, Gemini and Apollo programmes. It was used for timing critical engine burns, EVA activity, and even, famously, to help time re-entry procedures during the troubled Apollo 13 mission when onboard systems had failed.

The Speedmaster worn on the moon was the Speedmaster Professional ST105.012, featuring the now-iconic asymmetrical case (protective guards on the right side extended outwards to shield the crown and chronograph pusher), a manually wound calibre 321 movement, and a black dial with luminous markers and hands. The photograph of the watch fixed to Aldrin's wrist (with an extra-long strap to fit over the spacesuit) as he stood on the surface of the moon, is one of the most iconic images in horological history. Armstrong also walked the surface of the moon, but left his Speedmaster in the cockpit, as it was being used as a backup for a malfunctioning on-board timer – proof that the watches earned their place on the mission.

In the decades that followed, the Speedmaster continued to accompany astronauts on missions aboard Skylab, the Space Shuttle and even the International Space Station. To this day, it remains the only watch flight-qualified by NASA for EVA (extravehicular activity).

The Moon landing transformed the Speedmaster from a timing tool into a symbol of exploration, courage and humankind's ability to reach beyond limits. The brand had created a watch that was not only capable of surviving one of the most hostile environments known to man, but a watch that could be trusted when human lives depended on it.

Omega has continued to honour this legacy through special Moonwatch editions and partnerships linked to space exploration; all inspired by that first moment in 1969 when a mechanical chronograph joined the greatest human adventure of the 20th century.

OPPOSITE: Buzz Aldrin on the moon, wearing an Omega strapped to the outside of his suit, during the Apollo 11 mission. (Image courtesy of NASA)

RIGHT: The 1969 Alaska 1 prototype watch.

OPPOSITE: A replica NASA space suit at the Omega Museum in Biel/Bienne, Switzerland.

The Alaska Project

In the late 1960s and 1970s, Omega developed a series of experimental Speedmasters under the codename Alaska Project, with a view to creating the ultimate space watch for NASA. What did the watches have to do with Alaska? Absolutely nothing. It was chosen as a covert name that would confuse anyone outside of the project who happened to hear about it.

The goal was to enhance the Speedmaster's performance in out-of-this-world conditions, particularly the extreme temperatures of outer space. These prototypes featured oversized titanium or anodised aluminium outer cases, known as thermal shields, designed to protect the movement from both searing heat and deep cold.

Though never officially adopted by NASA, the Alaska Project showcased Omega's commitment to innovation beyond Earth's atmosphere. In 2008, Omega released a limited-edition Alaska Project Speedmaster (1,970 pieces), paying tribute to the original concept with a white dial and removable red aluminium outer case, echoing the experimental spirit of the original prototypes.

The Snoopy Speedmasters

While the Moon landing made the Speedmaster legendary, it was the events of the Apollo 13 mission that secured its status as a watch of remarkable reliability. Apollo 13 was NASA's third planned moon-landing mission, but it was dramatically aborted after an oxygen tank exploded, forcing the crew to improvise a perilous return to Earth using limited power and life support. The danger of the mission was captured in the 1995 blockbuster film *Apollo 13*.

With the spacecraft's digital timing systems compromised, the astronauts used an Omega Speedmaster chronograph to manually time a critical 14-second engine burn – a manoeuvre that helped realign the craft's trajectory for a safe return to Earth. In recognition of Omega's vital contribution to the mission's safe return, NASA astronauts awarded the brand the Silver Snoopy Award in 1970 – a rare honour given to those who go above and beyond in ensuring flight safety. The award is named after the *Peanuts* cartoon dog in honour of the Apollo 10 mission, the objective of which was to 'snoop around' the lunar surface to identify potential landing spots for the Apollo 11 crew.

Decades later, Omega would transform that moment of gratitude into a series of now-iconic timepieces, the Snoopy Speedmasters. The first, released in 2003, was a classic Moonwatch dial with a small illustration of Snoopy in the subdial at 9 o'clock. It has since become a cult favourite.

By 2015, Omega fully embraced the charm of its NASA-endorsed beagle with a white-dial model featuring Snoopy and a sterling silver caseback medallion with a detailed engraving of the Silver Snoopy Award insignia – Snoopy in a spacesuit, floating against a background of deep blue enamel. It was limited to just 1,970 pieces.

In 2020, Omega marked the 50th anniversary of its award with the Speedmaster Silver Snoopy Award 50th Anniversary – a feat of horological ingenuity thanks to an animated caseback. When the chronograph is activated, you can watch Snoopy orbit the moon aboard his Command Module, while just behind him the Earth completes a full spin. The words 'Eyes on the Stars' are written above.

This technical and visually poetic marvel, powered by Omega's Co-Axial Master Chronometer movement, proves that even the most serious tool watches can have a sense of humour, and a heart.

OPPOSITE: The caseback of the Speedmaster 'Silver Snoopy Award' 50th Anniversary watch shows Snoopy travelling through space.

ABOVE: This Speedmaster was created to mark the 50th anniversary the Snoopy Award, and features Snoopy in his space suit on the dial at 9 o'clock.

Dark Side of the Moon

In 2013, Omega launched the stealthy matte-black Speedmaster Dark Side of the Moon watch. It was a dramatic reimagining of the Moonwatch legacy that paid tribute to the Apollo 8 mission, whose astronauts became the first humans to see the far side of the moon not visible from Earth.

The case, bezel, crown and pushers of the watch were all crafted from a single block of black zirconium oxide ceramic; a material that is extremely tough, scratch resistant and lightweight. The watch updated the chronograph functionality of the classic Moonwatch with a dual-register chronograph display, 60-hour power reserve and automatic Co-Axial movement.

Following the success of the original, Omega expanded the Dark Side of the Moon collection with a series of bold variations. These included the 2015 Sedna Black with 18-carat gold details, 2016's grey-toned Meteorite with a meteorite dial, and the 2018 Apollo 8, which features a skeletonised dial, laser-etched lunar surface-inspired dial and small-seconds hand shaped like the Saturn V space rocket.

OPPOSITE TOP: Omega Speedmaster Dark Side of the Moon, ref 310.92.44.50.01.001.

OPPOSITE BOTTOM: The Dark Side of the Moon's specially decorated Omega Co-Axial Master Chronometer Calibre 3869 (left) and skeletonised black anodised aluminium dial.

ABOVE: The small-seconds subdial has a grade 5 titanium hand shaped like the Saturn V rocket.

Timing the Olympics

For nearly a century, Omega has stood at the finish line of the world's greatest sporting event. Since being appointed Official timekeeper of the Olympic Games in 1932, Omega has revolutionised the way athletic achievement is measured, setting new standards in accuracy from the running track to the swimming pool.

Omega's Olympic journey began at the Los Angeles 1932 Games, where a single technician arrived with 30 stopwatches to time every event. That modest beginning would lay the foundation for a legacy that has grown into a complex timekeeping operation involving tonnes of equipment, hundreds of trained specialists and cutting-edge digital timing systems.

Omega also became the official timekeeper for the Winter Olympics in 1936 at the Garmisch-Partenkirchen games. It has continued to be the official timekeeper for numerous Winter Olympics since then, including Pyeongchang 2018, Beijing 2022, and Milano Cortina 2026.

Among its most influential contributions to sports timing is the invention of the first photo-finish camera, which was introduced at the 1948 Olympics in London. This breakthrough allowed judges to see the exact moment athletes crossed the finish line, therefore no longer having to rely on the human eye to decide the winner in a close race.

With this advancement, the age of subjective timing was over. In the decades that followed, Omega pioneered innovations that became crucial to modern competition, including the electronic starting pistol, fully automatic timing (where the start and finish of a race are recorded without any human input), and sensor-equipped touchpads for swimming events that allow athletes to stop their own time with a tap at the wall.

OPPOSITE: An official Omega watch created for the London 2012 Olympics.

ABOVE: Omega created a countdown clock for the Milano Cortina 2026 Paralympic Winter Games.

Each advancement has served the same goal: to measure performance with absolute precision, ensuring every result is accurate and indisputable. This is especially important in an arena where medals can be decided by thousandths of a second.

In 1992, Omega extended its partnership with the Olympics by becoming Official timekeeper of the Paralympic Games, and also became Official timekeeper of the Youth Olympic Games in 2010.

Beyond timing technology, Omega's presence at the Olympic events can be observed in its distinctive red branding and countdown clocks, which have become much-loved fixtures in host cities. Omega also releases commemorative timepieces for each edition of the Games. The Paris 2024 Olympic and Paralympic collection included watches with themed design details including engraved casebacks with illustrations of the Games' iconic flame and rings, and Paris 2024 logos.

Perhaps Omega's greatest contribution to sport is its commitment to innovation in timing. With each Games, it pushes the boundaries of what timing can be, exploring new frontiers in motion sensors, real-time data and AI-driven analytics. At the Paris 2024 Games, for example, Omega introduced computer vision systems that utilise high-definition cameras and AI models to track athletes and objects, providing detailed performance metrics without the need for wearable sensors.

As sport evolves, Omega evolves with it, always finding new ways to honour athletes' endeavours with timing technology that can keep up with them.

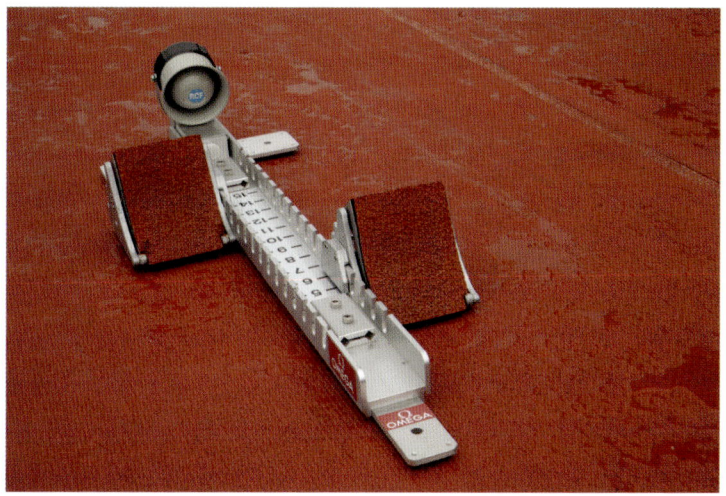

OPPOSITE: Omega branding on a bobsleigh at the Vancouver 2010 Olympics.

ABOVE: A starting block that uses Omega technology to time Olympic runners.

The Deepest Dive

In 2019, Omega redefined the limits of dive watch engineering with the Seamaster Planet Ocean Ultra Deep, a prototype timepiece that accompanied explorer Victor Vescovo on a record-breaking descent to the bottom of the Mariana Trench, the deepest point in Earth's oceans.

Three prototype watches were involved in the mission: two were fixed to the robotic arms of the DSV Limiting Factor submersible, and one was attached to a data-gathering unit called a 'lander'. All three watches withstood the Mariana Trench's immense pressure at a depth of 10,927 metres and returned to the surface fully functional.

Crafted from forged titanium, with a caseback designed to mimic the submersible's viewport, and a sapphire crystal nearly three times thicker than standard, the Ultra Deep wasn't a traditional commercial dive watch; it was a purpose-built prototype created to prove what was possible. It used technology developed in collaboration with the submersible's engineering team, bridging deep-sea exploration and horology expertise.

At the bottom of the Mariana Trench, the watches were subjected to more than 1,000 times atmospheric pressure. It is a hostile environment that few materials, let alone mechanical devices, can survive. The Ultra Deep watch on the lander was subjected to an even more rigorous ordeal than the other two, as due to a malfunction it became detached and stayed at the bottom of the ocean for an additional 52 hours under 16,000 psi of pressure before being retrieved. When tested on the surface, it was functioning normally and had only lost one second of accuracy.

Following the mission, Omega refined the design for wearability, and in 2022 it introduced a production version of the Ultra Deep, which was water-resistant to 6,000 metres and certified to ISO standards for saturation diving.

OPPOSITE: The Omega Seamaster Planet Ocean Ultra Deep watch created for Victor Vescovo.

LEFT: The forged titanium caseback of the Seamaster Planet Ocean Ultra Deep.

Licensed to Thrill

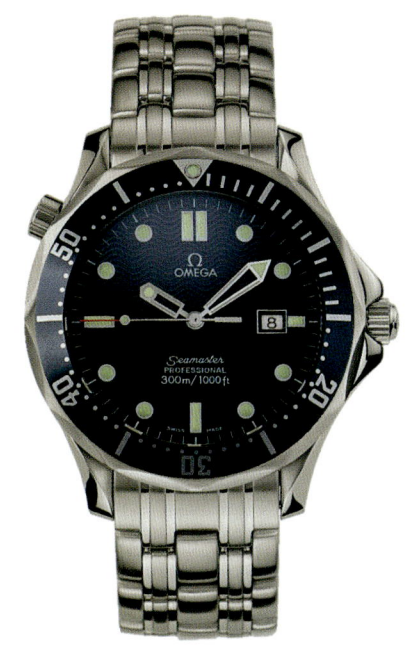

With the 1995 film *GoldenEye*, a new era of James Bond began. After a six-year hiatus, the franchise was back, with a new Bond in Pierce Brosnan and a new watch: the Omega Seamaster Diver 300M.

Previous Bonds had worn watches by Rolex, TAG Heuer, Hamilton, Seiko and others, but there had never been an affiliation. This changed with *GoldenEye* as Omega became the official watch of the world's favourite spy.

The decision to place a Seamaster on Bond's wrist was due to a shared naval heritage. The back story of Ian Fleming's character tells that he was a Commander in the Royal Naval Volunteer Reserve before becoming 007, while the Seamaster was originally developed as a tool watch for military divers and was issued to Royal Navy personnel.

OPPOSITE: Pierce Brosnan at Pinewood Studios in 1999, announcing that James Bond would wear the Omega Seamaster Professional Diver in *The World is Not Enough*.

ABOVE: Omega Seamaster Diver from the 1997 Bond film *Tomorrow Never Dies*.

Over the years, the partnership deepened, and Bond's horological tastes evolved. Brosnan's Bond was tooled up with gadget-equipped models, often including Q-added elements such as lasers and detonators. Daniel Craig, who played Bond from 2006 to 2021, had more varied tastes that included watches from the Diver, Planet Ocean and Aqua Terra families.

Omega began creating special James Bond editions, incorporating visual nods to the character, including the 007 logo, gun barrel motifs and the Bond family crest. Often these spy-inspired watches would be limited in number, making them highly collectible. None more so that the actual watches created for use in the films, such as the Omega Seamaster Diver 300M 007 Edition with a brown dial and mesh bracelet (designed with input from Craig) and crafted in titanium to withstand the rigours of filming action scenes. The original worn on set sold at auction at Christie's in 2022 for £226,800, with a commercial run of 7,007 more released onto the market.

OPPOSITE: Daniel Craig wears an Omega to an event to celebrate 60 years of James Bond.

ABOVE: Seamaster Diver 300m created to mark the 60th anniversary of James Bond.

Innovations

Omega's history is defined as much by innovation as by design. From early efforts to industrialise movement production to modern developments in anti-magnetic technology and escapement design, the brand has continually adapted to meet the technical demands of modern watchmaking. Some advances, like the Co-Axial escapement, aimed to improve mechanical efficiency and reduce wear over time, while others focused on resilience, responding to real-world challenges in sport, science, and exploration. These are the key innovations that shaped Omega.

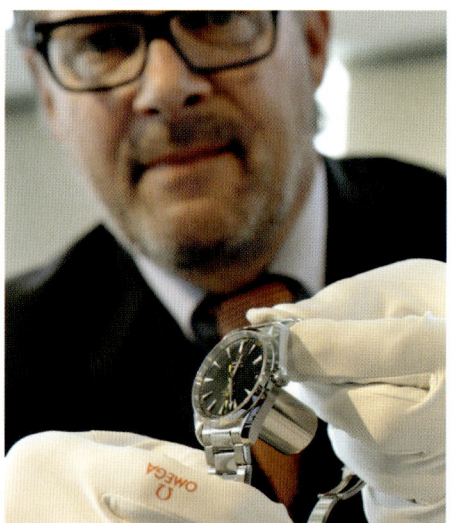

LEFT: Omega vice president and head of product development Jean-Claude Monachon in 2013 with the anti-magnetic Seamaster Aqua Terra 15000 Gauss.

OPPOSITE: A Noughties advert promoting the Omega Co-Axial movement.

The OMEGA Co-Axial Escapement
A Revolution in Master Watchmaking

Power reserve indication
3 year extended warranty

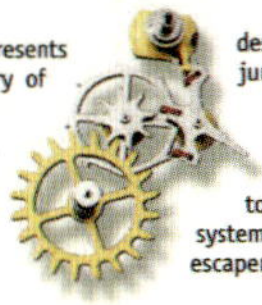

At the dawn of the third millennium, OMEGA presents an innovation that redefines the entire theory of mechanical watchmaking.

The escapement is the heart of every mechanical watch and the basic theory behind it has remained unchanged for over 200 years. Today, OMEGA breaks the mould with a totally new design, the Co-Axial Escapement, developed in conjunction with master watchmaker George Daniels.

The new design is based on a double co-axial escape wheel, a lever with three pallet stones and an impulse stone on the balance roller, together with a free sprung-balance. The co-axial system reduces sliding friction compared with the lever escapement and thus ensures greater accuracy over time.

www.omegawatches.com

The First Dive Watch

Long before diving watches became de rigeur for any serious watch brand, as they are today, Omega was experimenting with how to keep time underwater. In 1932, the brand launched the Omega Marine, which is widely regarded as the first commercially available dive watch.

Looking at the original model, you can hardly guess its function. It has a small Art Deco-style dial, more akin to a dress watch than the oversized, superluminova-laden dials that aid legibility in modern diver's watches. But there are clues: its brown leather strap featured an adjustable function that was new at that time, to allow it slip over wetsuits.

ABOVE: A 1937 advert for the Omega Marine watch.

OPPOSITE: Captain Yves le Prieur of the French Navy, pictured in 1926 wearing the revolutionary diving aparatus that he invented.

The real innovation of the Marine was an innovative double-case construction with an inner watch case that slid into a separate outer case. The cases were fixed to opposite ends of the extendable strap, creating a water-resistant seal when locked together.

This approach offered far greater protection than anything available at the time. Omega tested the Marine in both laboratory and real-world settings, most notably submerging it in Lake Geneva to a depth of 73 metres. Five years later, more extensive tests revealed that it could withstand depths of 135 metres. The watch quickly drew the attention of underwater adventurers. One of its early adopters was Yves Le Prieur, an officer in the French Navy and inventor of the open circuit Self-Contained Underwater Breathing Apparatus – or scuba, as we abbreviate it today. Another was the oceanographer and author Jacques Cousteau, who was the inspiration for the 2004 Wes Anderson film *The Life Aquatic* with Steve Zissou.

Though later eclipsed by round-cased models like the Seamaster, the Marine laid the groundwork for what a professional underwater watch could be. Its combination of innovative sealing, pressure resistance and field-tested durability established a blueprint that Omega – and the broader industry – would follow in the decades to come.

OPPOSITE: A French-language advert created for the Marine in 1937 targeting sailors.

RIGHT: An original Omega Marine wristwatch circa 1932.

The First Tourbillon Movement

In 1947, Omega produced a watchmaking milestone that was as discreet as it was radical. The brand developed the calibre 30I – the first tourbillon movement created specifically for a wristwatch. Unlike today's tourbillons, which are often showcased as visual centrepieces, this wasn't designed to be seen. Its purpose was not to wow collectors but to help it to compete in observatory timing trials, where mechanical precision was tested under strict conditions. A tourbillon is a rotating cage that holds a movement's escapement and balance wheel to counteract the effects of gravity on the regulating parts of the watch and therefore guarantee precision.

The tourbillon was invented by Abraham-Louis Breguet in 1795, but wasn't scaled down for a wristwatch until Omega's calibre 30I. It introduced a central tourbillon small enough for watches, engineered to make a full rotation every 60 seconds.

Just 12 of these experimental movements were produced, all hand-finished and adjusted for accuracy. They were never commercially available as the watches that housed them were built solely for chronometric competitions rather than for retail. Despite their low profile, these tourbillons delivered remarkable results, achieving high marks at observatory trials in Geneva and Neuchâtel.

Though Omega would not return to the tourbillon in a commercial wristwatch until decades later, the calibre 30I remains a landmark in the brand's technical history.

ABOVE: A watch case fitted with the Omega 301, the first tourbillon wristwatch calibre in the world.

LEFT: The reverse shows the workings of this movement, which dates back to 1947.

An Early Swiss Quartz Movement

By the late 1960s, the watch industry was on the edge of a technological shift that would come to define the next two decades. Japanese brand Seiko was snapping at the heels of the Swiss watch industry, creating ever-more accurate mechanical watches and even taking Omega's role as official Olympic timekeeper at the 1964 Tokyo Games, at which it used timers powered by quartz movements.

The rise of quartz timekeeping – electronic battery-charged movements powered by vibrating quartz crystals – promised levels of accuracy that far exceeded mechanical calibres. They were also cheaper. For Swiss watchmakers, quartz movements posed a threat, but also an opportunity.

Seiko released the world's first quartz wristwatch, the Astron, in 1969, and Omega was quick to respond with its own. It launched the Omega Electroquartz at the Schweizer Mustermesse Basel watch fair in 1970. The Electroquartz was powered by the Beta 21 movement, developed by a consortium of 20 Swiss watch brands through the Centre Electronique Horloger (CEH) in Neuchâtel. Many other Swiss brands launched Beta 21-powered quartz models at the 1970 fair, including Rolex, Patek Philippe and IWC.

Early Omega Electroquartz watches featured bold, asymmetrical gold cases, with the crown on the left-side, and a champagne dial marked with Electroquartz. Rather than shy away from fact that it was using quartz movements, Omega leaned in. A 1975 advert for the later Megaquartz 2400 model shows the innards of a circuit board, describing it as "beautiful".

OPPOSITE: The 1974 Omega Megaquartz 2400 Marine Chronometer.

ABOVE: A 1970 Omega Constellation Electroquart with a quartz movement.

Though the Beta 21 would be short-lived – soon replaced by smaller, more efficient quartz calibres – it represented a pivotal moment in Swiss watchmaking. Omega had taken an early and active role in embracing electronic timekeeping, not as a replacement for mechanical craftsmanship but as a parallel innovation.

In the decade that followed the optimistic launch at the Basel fair, the watch industry would be shaken by what became known as the Quartz Crisis, as low-cost quartz watches from Asia flooded global markets, pushing many traditional brands to the brink.

LEFT: The Omega Constellation Megaquartz 2400, launched in 1974.

OPPOSITE: A 1976 advert created to promote Omega's quartz-powered marine chronometer.

The only marine chronometer wristwatch in the world.

An Omega Quartz.

The extraordinary precision that was brought to us by the quartz crystals was discovered by Omega a long time ago.

We introduced the electronic chronometric quartz system as far back as 1952 at the Helsinki Olympic games. Since then, we've been constantly improving it.

For us at Omega, there is something even more important than accuracy or precision alone. It is the constancy of that precision, otherwise known as reliability.

You will find this reliability, tested in competition, in the Omega Quartz that you wear. It allows for a time discrepancy of only one second per month. Reliability which has enabled Omega to perfect the first wristwatch in the world that is authorized as a marine chronometer by observatories. So place your faith in your Omega Quartz, the watch that has earned it.

The Co-Axial Escapement

ABOVE: A sketch of the Co-Axial movement.

In 1999, Omega released the Co-Axial escapement, a mechanical innovation developed by English watchmaker George Daniels. The Co-Axial escapement reduces friction between the movement's components, particularly in the area where energy is transferred from the mainspring to the balance wheel. By separating the locking and impulse functions onto different surfaces, the system eliminates the sliding contact that typically causes wear and demands regular lubrication, thus ensuring that watches are more accurate for longer, and require less servicing.

Although Daniels had come up with this groundbreaking horological invention in the 1970s, he had done so at a time when the Swiss watch industry was focused on quartz movements, first creating them and then dealing with the fallout as mechanical sales declined. As such, Daniels made several wasted trips to Switzerland to show his escapement to the major brands. None were interested; although Patek Philippe did request that Daniels convert one of its Nautilus watches with his Co-Axial escapement as a prototype in 1981 – you can see this on display at The Science Museum in London.

Interestingly, Daniels had fitted his own early experimental Co-Axial escapement into the calibre 1045 of his personal Omega Speedmaster Mark 4.5, perhaps manifesting the deal that came in 1993. That year, Omega bought the patent for the Co-Axial escapement from Daniels, who worked with the brand for the next six years to perfect his invention before it was launched inside an Omega De Ville in 1999. The use of the Co-Axial escapement would gradually expand to other Omega collections, and now it is a main selling point for the brand.

ABOVE: George Daniels, the inventor of the Co-Axial movement.

Anti-Magnetic Movement

In 2013, Omega revealed a breakthrough that would quietly redefine the expectations of modern mechanical watchmaking. The brand introduced the world's first fully anti-magnetic movement. The Omega calibre 8508 was capable of resisting magnetic fields greater than 15,000 gauss – a level of protection far beyond anything previously seen in the watch industry.

While Omega's Railmaster and Rolex's Milgauss pioneered magnetic resistance through shielding in the 1950s, Omega's 2013 breakthrough was the first to eliminate the problem at the movement level by creating a calibre that was fully anti-magnetic by design, not by enclosure.

The solution lay in re-engineering the movement using non-ferrous materials, including silicon components and anti-magnetic alloys. By eliminating the parts most vulnerable to magnetism, Omega created a calibre that could maintain its accuracy and function in environments that would severely disrupt a conventional watch.

The first model to house this innovation was the Seamaster Aqua Terra >15,000 Gauss, featuring a movement that remained completely visible through a sapphire caseback, proving that anti-magnetism didn't have to come at the cost of aesthetics.

OPPOSITE: The Omega Seamaster Aqua Terra 15000 Gauss, pictured in 2013.

This advance laid the groundwork for a wider transformation. Omega's new-generation movements would soon be tested not only for traditional chronometric performance, but also for magnetic resistance, power reserve and robustness, all certified by the Swiss Federal Institute of Metrology (METAS) under the Master Chronometer standard.

In a world increasingly filled with magnetic fields – from smartphones and laptops to airport scanners – Omega's anti-magnetic calibres address a very modern challenge.

The Icons

From the watch worn on the moon to the models seen on the silver screen, Omega's most recognisable designs have become cherished models that collectors return to time and again. From the Speedmaster to the Seamaster, the Constellation and the De Ville, these iconic timepieces represent the pillars of Omega's legacy, with each one telling a different story. Whether a keen collector or simply curious, these are the names to know, and the references that continue to matter.

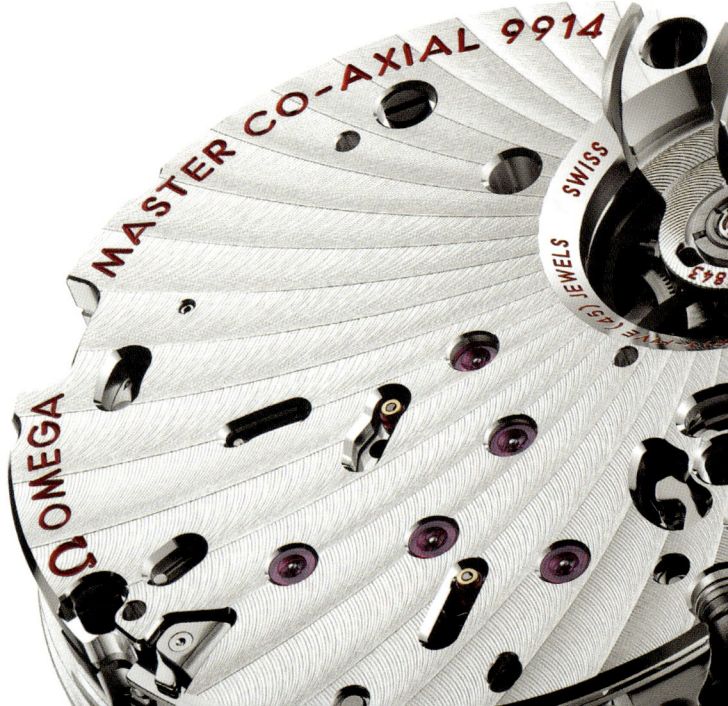

OPPOSITE: Omega's Master Co-Axial 9914 movement, which is used in its Speedmaster watches.

ABOVE: The De Ville Prestige in steel and Sedna gold.

Seamaster

The Seamaster is Omega's longest-running watch line, introduced in 1948 to mark the brand's 100th anniversary. Inspired by the rugged reliability of military watches used during World War II, the original Seamaster combined everyday wearability with water resistance, made possible by an O-ring gasket and a robust case design.

Early Seamasters were elegant by modern standards – slim, dressy timepieces designed more for splash resistance than deep-sea diving. That changed in the 1950s with the introduction of the Seamaster 300. Launched in 1957 as part of Omega's professional trilogy, alongside the Speedmaster and Railmaster, the Seamaster 300 was aimed squarely at serious divers. It featured a rotating bezel, high-contrast dial and superior water resistance, quickly gaining popularity among professionals.

In the decades that followed, the Seamaster evolved into a platform for experimentation. The 1970s brought the bold, asymmetrical Ploprof (short for *plongeurs professionnels*, French for 'professional divers'), developed with French deep-sea diving specialists. In 1993, the Seamaster Diver 300M introduced a new wave-pattern dial and helium escape valve, a design that would become closely linked with the James Bond franchise after its appearance in 1995's *GoldenEye*.

Today, the Seamaster collection continues to grow, ranging from vintage-inspired chronometers to ultra-modern ceramic dive watches. Despite their differences, all Seamasters carry a shared legacy of durability, precision and versatility that make them a great choice both above and below the surface.

OPPOSITE: The Seamaster 37mm in Moonshine gold on an alligator strap.

RIGHT: A close-up view of the Moonshine Gold pin buckle with Omega logo.

Constellation

The Constellation has been Omega's expression of precision and elegance since 1952. Launched to celebrate the brand's dominance in observatory chronometer trials, it was positioned as Omega's flagship watch, combining refined styling with accurate timekeeping. Early models featured a gold medallion on the caseback depicting an observatory beneath a starry sky. The eight stars in the caseback design represent Omega's record-setting achievements in trials.

These first-generation Constellations also introduced the now-iconic pie-pan dial – a 12-sided design with dial edges that slope down like an inverted dish. Originally a by-product of manufacturing, the shape quickly became a defining feature and remains a collector favourite.

The Constellation underwent a radical redesign in 1982 with the arrival of the Manhattan. It introduced an integrated bracelet, a barrel-shaped case, and four claws gripping the case at 3 o'clock and 9 o'clock. Originally, these claws were functional, pressing the crystal and gasket firmly against the case to improve water resistance. In later versions this was no longer required, but the claws remained as a stylistic signature. While the original Constellation was a classically proportioned dress watch, the Manhattan gave it a sharp, geometric identity that found a strong following in international markets, particularly across Asia. Today's models stay close to that blueprint, with polished facets, Roman numeral bezels and a wide range of case sizes and materials.

OPPOSITE TOP: Constellation in steel and Moonshine Gold, a PVD green dial with Supernova pattern.

OPPOSITE BOTTOM: Constellation watches with meteorite dials and diamond details on the hour markers and bezels.

ABOVE: A Constellation watch with a mono-rang bracelet in steel and 18-karat yellow gold (left), and another with a dial made from a piece of iron meteorite.

Ladymatic

When Omega introduced the Ladymatic in 1955, it marked one of the earliest attempts to create a women's watch that didn't compromise on mechanical innovation. While many brands were focused solely on styling for ladies' watches, Omega developed an entirely new movement, the calibre 455. It was one of the smallest automatic movements in the world at the time at just 17.5mm in diameter.

The original Ladymatic models were compact, rounded and classically feminine, with gold cases, delicate lugs and applied hour markers. They reflected the aesthetic of mid-Century fashion but were serious watches underneath. As the brand advertised in the 1950s, Ladymatics were "the world's smallest automatic chronometer watch", with ads in the American press pointing out they were "minuscule… no larger around than a dime". And in 1959, you could buy one for $115.

Unusually for the time, Omega ran dual campaigns for its men's watches and the Ladymatic, setting it apart as one of the few brands seriously investing in mechanical innovation for women.

Omega continued producing the line for nearly two decades before quietly retiring it in the 1970s as tastes shifted and quartz watches gained popularity. Then in 2010, the Ladymatic returned as part of the De Ville family of dress watches. The new designs kept the flowing, sculpted cases of the originals but scaled up. It also introduced a more contemporary palette of materials, including ceramic, mother-of-pearl, and diamond-set bezels. At its core was the calibre 8520, designed to fit case sizes of 32mm to 36mm.

OPPOSITE: A steel and gold Ladymatic watch with a snow-set diamond bezel.

Speedmaster

The Speedmaster might be best known for going to the moon, but its story began on the racetrack. Launched in 1957 as part of Omega's professional trilogy, alongside the Seamaster 300 and Railmaster, the original Speedmaster was designed for timing motor races. It was the first chronograph to feature a tachymeter scale on the bezel, rather than printed on the dial, allowing for better legibility while tracking speed.

Its transformation into a space icon began in the 1960s when NASA tested a range of chronographs for use in manned spaceflight. The Speedmaster outperformed all rivals in a series of extreme conditions (heat, cold, vibration, vacuum) and in 1965 it was flight-qualified for all NASA missions – a seal of approval that the Speedmaster Professional models hold to this day. That same year, it was worn during the Gemini 4 spacewalk by astronaut Ed White, and in 1969 it became the first watch worn on the Moon during Apollo 11, earning it the sobriquet of Moonwatch.

It is important to note, however, that not all Speedmasters are Moonwatches. The term specifically refers to the models that follow the design of the NASA-certified manual-wind chronographs, including references 105.012 and 145.012 and their modern variations.

Beyond the Moonwatch, the Speedmaster expanded into numerous sub-lines, including the automatic Speedmaster Reduced, the Mark series, the 38mm collection, and the Speedmaster '57. Limited editions also play a central role, such as the Silver Snoopy Award pieces celebrating Omega's part in the Apollo 13 mission, and the Moonshine Gold Apollo 11 50th Anniversary edition.

While the Speedmaster has adapted to changing tastes, its design language has remained remarkably consistent: a black dial, three-register chronograph layout and tool-like legibility.

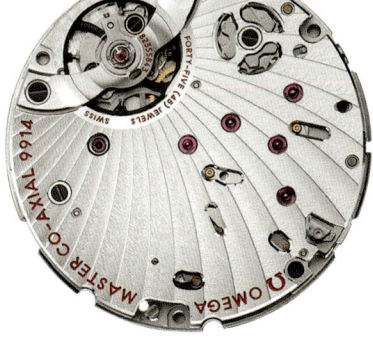

OPPOSITE: A Speedmaster Moonphase with a galvanic grey-coated meteorite plate dial.

ABOVE: The Master Co-Axial 9914 calibre that powers Omega's Speedmaster watches.

Railmaster

The Railmaster was introduced in 1957 as a tool watch for people who worked around magnetic fields. It was aimed at scientists, engineers and railway staff; anyone whose profession could interfere with a watch's accuracy due to high levels of magnetism. Omega built the Railmaster to resist up to 1,000 gauss, using a soft iron inner case and dial to shield the movement. It launched alongside the Seamaster 300 and Speedmaster as part of Omega's professional trilogy.

The design of the watch was clean and functional. The original reference CK2914 featured a matte black dial, broad arrow hands and luminous triangular hour markers. There was no date and minimal text. A printed minute track circled the dial.

The Railmaster was discontinued in 1963 after just six years. It is thought that this was due to weaker sales than the other two professional watches. However – as is often the case with rare and discontinued watches – it found cult status among collectors on the secondary market. In 2018, an original 1957 Railmaster CK2914-4 sold at Phillips New York for $45,000.

ABOVE: An Omega Seamaster Railmaster Co-Axial Master Chronometer.

OPPOSITE: The watch has bold triangular hour markers on the dial filled with light-grey Super-LumiNova.

In 2003, Omega revived the Railmaster, bringing out updated designs that retained the original model's anti-magnetic inner case. Though it enjoyed a longer run than the original model, the Railmaster of the Noughties was discontinued again in 2012.

The Railmaster was given a third shot in 2017, as part of wider celebrations to mark the 60th anniversary of Omega's professional trilogy. These limited-edition models were powered by the Master Chronometer-certified calibre 8806, which uses non-ferrous components – including a silicon balance spring – to achieve magnetic resistance without the need for a protective inner case. This brought the Railmaster in line with Omega's broader push toward anti-magnetic innovation across its core collections, offering an increased resistance of more than 15,000 gauss.

The modern Railmaster enjoyed some years of success before being discontinued again in 2024. Whether it will make another comeback in the future remains to be seen, but for now this model can be found on the secondary market and within Omega's Heritage offering.

OPPOSITE: This version of the Railmaster has a denim strap as a nod to the clothing of railroad workers.

LEFT: The Railmaster Ref. 220-12-40-20-03-001 measures 40mm and has a brushed 'blue jeans' dial.

De Ville

The De Ville dress watch first surfaced in the early 1960s as a sub-line within the sporty Seamaster family, offering a more sophisticated look for onshore attire. In 1967, Omega launched the De Ville as a standalone collection, removing Seamaster from the dial. Early De Villes were beautifully simple dress watches, with round gold-tone cases, leather straps, sleek hour markers and a date window at 3 o'clock. The casebacks were engraved with a cityscape as a nod to the name of the model, which is French for 'city', and to its positioning as a chic urban dress watch.

In the 1970s, the De Ville achieved significant validation for its sleek design, picking up awards at the Grand Prix Triomphe de l'Excellence Européenne and Baden-Baden Design Awards. It was a time of experimentation for the model, with square and oval cases being added to the collection, and even a ladies' dress watch with an elongated octagon dial inspired by emerald-cut gemstones.

The collection embraced quartz movements in the 1970s and 1980s. Swapping to these movements allowed Omega's designers to create thinner cases, and to make the collection more affordable.

The De Ville collection has expanded over time into a series of sub-lines, each tailored to a different style or function. The De Ville Prestige is the most enduring, introduced in the 1990s as a classically styled dress watch line with clean dials, Roman numerals, and slim cases. The De Ville Hour Vision, launched in 2007, was created to showcase Omega's Co-Axial movement through a transparent sapphire case. The De Ville Ladymatic, revealed in 2010, was Omega's push to introduce high-end mechanical movements to women's watches.

OPPOSITE: A De Ville Prestige with a PVD blackened sun-brushed dial, which has a 'railway' minute track.

BELOW: The De Ville Prestige watches are available with steel bracelets or leather straps.

Diver 300M

The Seamaster Diver 300M redefined Omega's approach to the modern dive watch when it launched in 1993. While the Seamaster name had existed since 1948 and the Seamaster 300 since 1957, the Diver 300M was something different – a fully contemporary design with bold styling. Its scalloped bezel, skeletonised sword hands and signature wave-pattern dial set it apart visually, while technical features like a screw-down crown, unidirectional bezel and helium escape valve confirmed its underwater credentials.

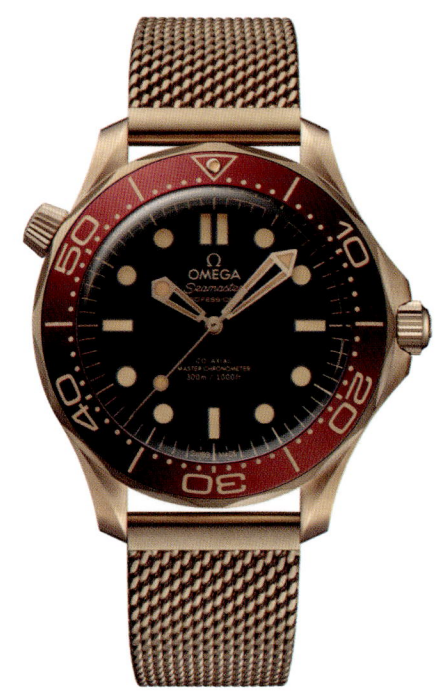

The watch was powered by a COSC-certified automatic movement and offered 300 metres of water resistance (hence the 300M name), positioning it firmly within the professional dive watch category. Yet it didn't feel purely utilitarian; polished accents, applied markers and that distinctive dial texture gave it a sense of refinement.

The balance of function and flair helped it break through culturally in 1995, when Pierce Brosnan wore the Seamaster Diver 300M as James Bond in *GoldenEye*. It was the beginning of a long-standing partnership between Omega and the James Bond franchise, with the Diver 300M featuring in *Tomorrow Never Dies*, *The World is Not Enough*, Die *Another Day*, and *Skyfall*.

The Diver 300M design has evolved over time, but the core elements remain. In 2018, Omega released an updated version with a ceramic dial, laser-engraved wave motif, and the brand's Co-Axial Master Chronometer movement.

OPPOSITE: The Seamaster Diver 300M in bronze gold, with a a burgundy oxalic anodised aluminium bezel ring.

ABOVE: The Seamster Diver 300M is waterproof to depths of up to 300 metres.

Aqua Terra

Introduced in 2002, the Seamaster Aqua Terra was created to sit between Omega's professional dive watches and its more formal collections. It was built with water resistance, anti-magnetism and robust construction, but styled for everyday wear. The name reflects its purpose – 'Aqua' for the sea, 'terra' for land – positioning it as a versatile companion for both.

Though it belongs to the Seamaster family, the Aqua Terra doesn't feature a dive bezel or helium escape valve, but it does have a water resistance rating of 150 metres. The modern Aqua Terra's most recognisable feature is its dial. Inspired by luxury yacht decking, the vertical or horizontal teak-pattern lines give the watch a strong nautical character without leaning too heavily into sporty aesthetics. The dial, which was first introduced in 2008 (earlier versions had vertical stripes), is paired with clean arrowhead markers and broad hands.

While James Bond wore the Diver 300M and Planet Ocean in films, Daniel Craig was often photographed off-set wearing an Aqua Terra, especially during the *Spectre* and *No Time to Die* press tours. This publicity helped to cement its position as a luxury sports watch you can wear with a suit.

Since 2017, all Aqua Terra models have featured Master Chronometer-certified movements, combining anti-magnetic resistance of over 15,000 gauss with precise timekeeping and durable construction.

The Aqua Terra is produced in a wide range of sizes and configurations. These include classic three-hand models, annual calendars, GMTs and watches with small seconds sub dials. It has been made in steel, Sedna gold, titanium and platinum, with dial colours ranging from classic black, blue and green, to champagne and linen-textured silver.

With its blend of sport and sophistication, the Aqua Terra has earned a reputation as one of Omega's most modern and versatile watches.

OPPOSITE: The Seamster Aqua Terra 150M in steel, with a lacquered black varnish dial.

LEFT: The watch has an integrated bracelet and is powered by Omeaga's Co-Axial Master Chronometer calibre 8800.

Constellation Globemaster

The Constellation Globemaster was introduced in 2015 as a bridge between past and present. The dress watch was inspired by early Omega Constellation models from the 1950s and 1960s. The naming of the watch also referenced a forgotten chapter of Omega's mid-century history. When Omega launched the Constellation line in the United States during the early 1950s, it faced a trademark conflict over the name so temporarily marketed some of its Constellation watches in the US under Globemaster – a name that later laid dormant until the launch of the 2015 Globemaster.

The most distinctive elements of the Globemaster's design are its pie-pan dial (a subtle 12-sided dial that recalls the earliest Constellation references) and a fluted bezel. The case design is clean and round, with brushed and polished finishes. In a departure from the more angular Manhattan-style Constellations, it has no claws.

Technically, the Globemaster was a milestone for Omega as it was the first watch to receive Master Chronometer certification, first introduced via a partnership with METAS in 2015. Its calibre 8900 (or 8901 in gold models) set new standards for magnetic resistance, accuracy and power reserve, all of which were tested under real-world conditions. The result was a watch that looked vintage, but contained cutting-edge horological innards.

The Globemaster has expanded beyond its original three-hand format to include a range of variations that reflect different functions and materials. In 2016, Omega introduced the Globemaster Annual Calendar, which tracks the months as well as the date (which is visible in a date window at 6 o'clock). The names of all 12 months are written in cursive script between the hour markers, and the current month is indicated by an additional hand.

OPPOSITE: A Constellation Globemaster in Sedna Gold with a sun-brushed blue Pie Pan dial.

LEFT: The caseback of this steel Constellation Globemaster has a Central Observatory medallion behind sapphire crystal.

Seamaster Planet Ocean

The Seamaster Planet Ocean was launched in 2005 as a more rugged, performance-driven alternative to the Diver 300M. Designed for professional and technical diving, it offered 600 metres of water resistance – double that of the Diver 300M – and featured a helium escape valve, unidirectional bezel and screw-down crown.

It was a bold statement of Omega's deep-sea capability, aimed at divers and collectors who wanted serious underwater credentials. This was reinforced by Victor Vescovo's 2019 Mariana Trench expedition, when specially built Planet Ocean Ultra Deep watches were strapped to the outside of the submersible, which travelled to a depth of 10,927 metres. This set a world record for the deepest dive by a mechanical watch.

The 2005 Planet Ocean models had large case sizes of 42mm and 45.5mm, with designs that nodded to the Seamaster 300 with broad arrow hands and Arabic numerals at the cardinal points (12, 3, 6 and 9 o'clock). The watches also had orange bezel accents, a colour that quickly became a visual signature for the line.

Over time, the collection expanded to include multiple sizes, materials and complications. Chronograph and GMT versions were introduced, along with limited editions tied to events such as the

Olympic Games and the James Bond franchise. Case materials have ranged from stainless steel and titanium to ceramic and Sedna gold, with dials and bezels produced in vibrant hues. Since 2015, all Planet Ocean models have been fitted with Master Chronometer-certified movements.

For Omega, Planet Ocean represents the cutting edge of its underwater expertise. It is a modern icon shaped by adventure, function, and the brand's ongoing commitment to pushing the limits below the surface of the waves.

OPPOSITE: Seamaster Planet Ocean 600M in black ceramic on a rubber strap.

LEFT: The caseback of the Seamaster Planet Ocean 600M, showing the Master Co-Axial 8938 movement.

De Ville Trésor

The De Ville Trésor was launched in 2014 as a sophisticated dress watch inspired by Omega's mid-Century archives. The name, which is French for 'treasure', first appeared in 1949 when Omega launched a line of elegant 18-karat gold dress watches with silvered dials, gold Arabic numerals and faceted, pear-shaped indexes.

The modern Trésor draws from that legacy, combining vintage-inspired styling with contemporary watchmaking standards. It stands out within the De Ville family as a more dressy and luxurious choice.

Its clean, domed sapphire glass, curved lugs and slender indices take inspiration from the 1949 model. It is also thinner that other De Ville models, with cases that can measure just 11mm. This makes it easier to wear underneath a dress shirt cuff, or as a chic evening watch for ladies.

Since its reintroduction, the Trésor has quietly expanded to include a full range of men's and women's models, with both manual-wind and automatic movements. There is a creative artistry to be found within this collection, with Omega's designers playing with strap colours, dial designs and diamond accents.

In 2021, Omega introduced the Mini Trésor, a dedicated line of women's models with quartz movements in a compact 26mm case. These watches reinterpret the Trésor concept with fun aesthetics such as floral or patterned dials, double-wrap straps and solid 18-karat Moonshine gold editions.

The growing range of Trésor models shows how Omega can merge vintage cues with modern style, and create fun, fashion-forward dress watches that balance out its sportier offerings.

OPPOSITE: De Ville Mini Trésor with a Toile de Jouy double-wrap strap with a blue and white sea-inspired design.

ABOVE: A single diamond is set in the crown of the De Ville Mini Trésor, surrounded by a red ceramic floral motif.

Swiss Made

More than a mark of origin, the words Swiss Made speak to a tradition of precision, craftsmanship and enduring value. Being Swiss Made means drawing from centuries of horological expertise whilst simultaneously pushing the boundaries of what watchmaking can be. From its roots in La Chaux-de-Fonds to its advanced production facilities in Biel/Bienne, Omega has remained a central figure in the story of Swiss watchmaking through its commitment to innovation, integrity, and horological excellence.

ABOVE: A watchmaker at the Omega factory shows the different components that go into one of its calibres.

OPPOSITE: A sunset view of the Omega factory at Biel/Bienne, which opened in 2017.

The Manufacture

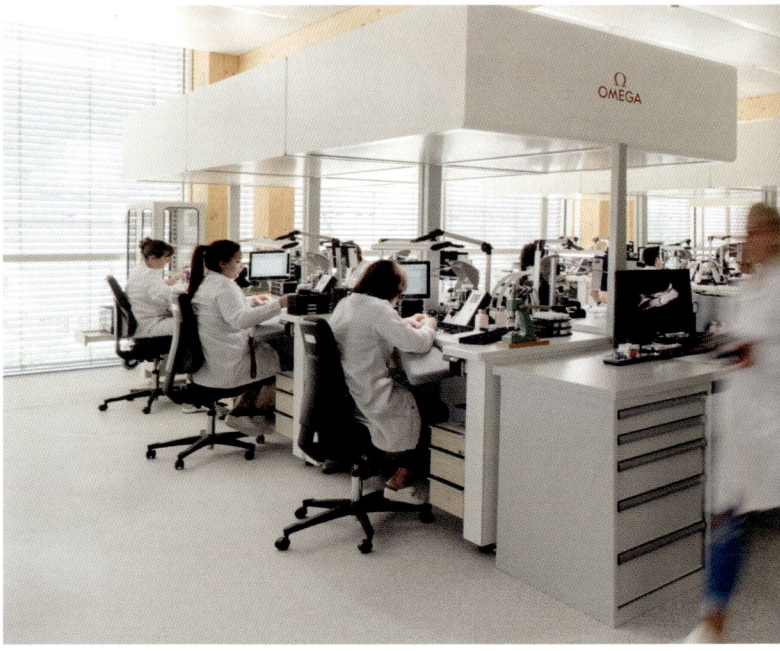

Omega's manufacturing operations are rooted in the town of Biel/Bienne, a bilingual hub in the Swiss Jura mountains that has been home to the watchmaker since 1880. In 2017, Omega opened a state-of-the-art facility in the city that brought together the key stages of watch production, from assembly to shipping, under one roof, continuing Omega's legacy of efficiency and watchmaking at scale. The purpose-built manufacture also addressed the problem faced by its previous network of workshops housed in heritage, protected buildings that could not easily be modified for the growing needs of the watchmaker.

LEFT: Watchmakers on the floor of Omega's manufacture in Switzerland.

The 172,225 square foot, five-storey building was designed by award-winning Japanese architect Shigeru Ban with sustainability at its core. This is evident as soon as you walk through the front doors, as you will notice that the building is crafted from locally sourced wooden beams of Swiss spruce constructed using a wooden dowel system with no metal fastenings. Heating and cooling are powered by geothermal systems, which reduce the need for conventional heating and air conditioning, and it has solar panels that contribute to the building's energy supply. Such innovations have ensured that it meets Minergie standards, a Swiss certification for low-energy consumption buildings.

Inside, the space is highly automated. One of the most notable features is the central storage tower housing 26,000 boxes filled with Omega components, which will be used to build the 700,000 watches Omega produces each year. It is manned by a group of four bright-yellow robot pickers – named by staff as John, George, Paul, and Ringo, after The Beatles. Every time a watchmaker needs a part, the robot pickers will dash to the right box to retrieve and deliver it. You can see them at work through glass windows in the foyer of the factory.

The building also houses Omega's METAS Master Chronometer testing facility, where watches undergo rigorous certification beyond traditional COSC standards. Each timepiece is exposed to magnetic fields of 15,000 gauss, tested in various positions and temperatures and measured for precision, water resistance and power reserve. These real-world simulations set the benchmark for modern chronometry and are central to Omega's identity today.

While Biel/Bienne is the core of Omega's watchmaking activities, the brand's manufacturing network extends beyond a single site. It operates additional facilities nearby, including one dedicated to the production of ceramic components used in bezels and case parts. Omega also benefits from its place within the Swatch Group ecosystem, often leaning on the production of other factories for specialist items. It also has a factory 30 kilometres away in Villeret dedicated primarily to the assembly of its mechanical movements. Once the movements are built, they are shipped to the Biel/Bienne manufacture to be assembled in its watches.

Watchmaker training also takes place in-house at Biel/Bienne, with Omega supporting professional development through its own programmes, as well as institutions like WOSTEP.

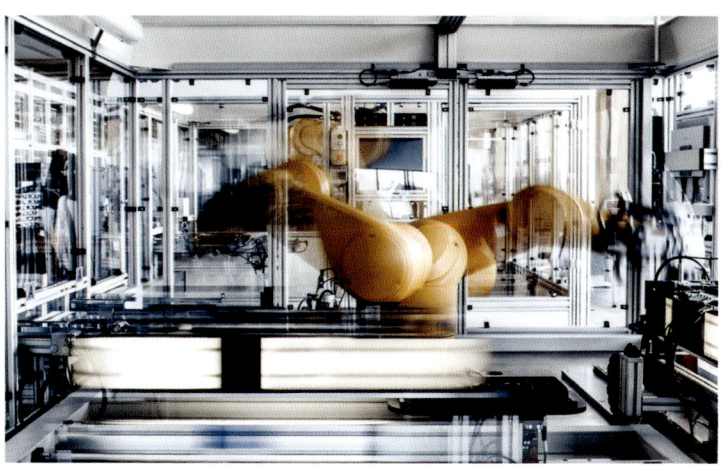

OPPOSITE: The storage towers in the Omega factory, which are attended to by robot pickers.

ABOVE: A robotic arm at work, which is used for repetitive tasks such as winding watches.

Movements

Omega's in-house movement production started in 1894, when it introduced the serially produced 19-ligne 'Omega' calibre that gave the company its name. While Omega relied on ETA movements for much of the late 20th century (Swatch Group purchased the well-known movement maker in 1985), the brand began reasserting technical independence in 1999 with the introduction of the Co-Axial escapement.

The Co-Axial escapement, developed by British watchmaker George Daniels, sought to reduce friction in the movement's regulating organ, offering better long-term timekeeping and less need for maintenance.

This led to the launch of the calibre 8500 in 2007 – the first modern Omega movement designed entirely in-house to accommodate the Co-Axial system. Since then, Omega has steadily expanded its in-house movement programme.

Contemporary Omega movements feature silicon balance springs as standard, anti-magnetic materials, and offer solid power reserves. A key feature of Omega movements are the laser-etched arabesque Geneva waves (a signature spiral-style finishing pattern) on the larger components, which are often visible through exhibition casebacks.

OPPOSITE: A deconstructed Omega movement at the Biel/Bienne factory.

LEFT: An Omega Co-Axial 8400 calibre gets a tweak from a qualified watchmaker.

Precision

Precision has defined Omega's watchmaking for more than a hundred years. In the early 20th century, the brand made its name at international observatory trials – competitive timekeeping contests held in places like Geneva, Neuchâtel, and the King's Royal Observatory at Kew in England. Omega regularly topped the rankings, setting records for mechanical accuracy that helped cement its reputation as a leader in chronometry.

Observatory trials were serious technical benchmarks, and Omega used them to test and refine its calibres, feeding improvements back into production watches. This focus on accuracy became part of the company's DNA.

In 2015, Omega teamed up with METAS, the Swiss Federal Institute of Metrology, to launch its Master Chronometer certification. METAS is Switzerland's official body for measuring standards, and is responsible for ensuring accuracy and consistency in scientific and industrial measurements across fields such as time, temperature and mass.

OPPOSITE: This certificate is sold with all Omega watches that have been deemed Master Chronometers by METAS.

ABOVE: An Omega Master Co-Axial 8700 movement.

The partnership between Omega and METAS marked a significant step forward in watch testing standards, shifting the focus from just the movement to the performance of the entire finished watch. It was developed as a response to real-world demands, with the certification designed to test what matters most to everyday wearers: precision, durability, and resistance to external influences.

The Master Chronometer process includes eight rigorous tests over a 10-day period. These assess timekeeping accuracy in multiple positions and temperatures, power reserve, water resistance and resistance to magnetism. Each watch must continue to function within a tolerance of 0 to +5 seconds per day, even after exposure to magnetic fields of 15,000 gauss, a level far beyond what most people encounter in daily life.

Unlike COSC certification, which only tests uncased movements, the METAS process evaluates the completed watch as it will be worn. Every certified timepiece receives an individual results report, viewable via a QR code included with the watch.

The certification reflects Omega's efforts to create standards that go beyond industry norms. Today, the Master Chronometer label appears across the brand's core collections, from the Aqua Terra and Speedmaster to the Constellation and Globemaster.

OPPOSITE: A watchmaker examines the final finish on a watch bracelet.

BELOW: Applique details such as the Omega symbol are applied to the dial by hand.

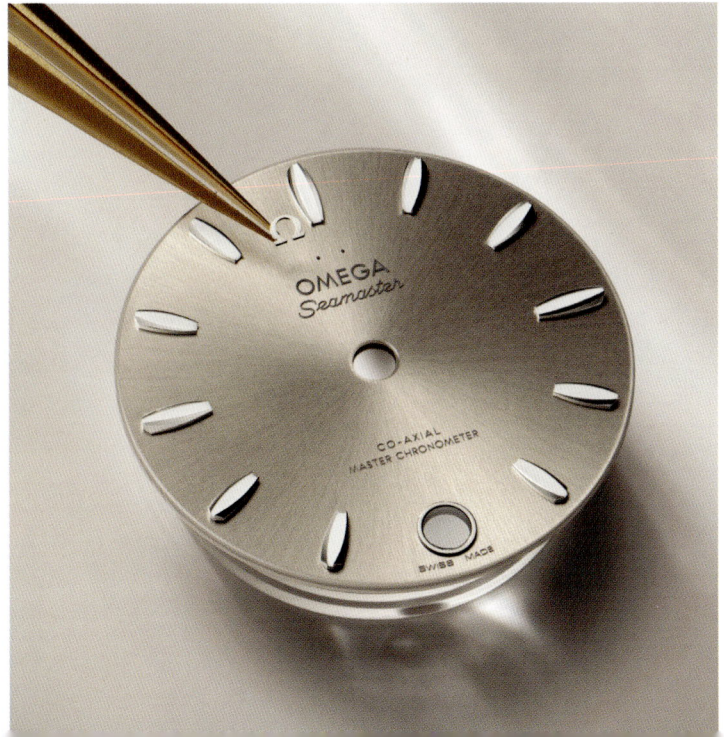

ABOVE: A robotic arm gets ready to pack an Omega Master Chronometer certificate into a watch box.

Testing

Before it leaves the manufacture, every Omega watch undergoes a series of demanding tests to ensure it meets the brand's internal standards for performance, durability and reliability. These checks are designed to simulate both everyday wear and more extreme conditions, reflecting the environments Omega watches have historically been exposed to, from ocean depths to polar expeditions and the unknowns of outer space.

The testing process covers a range of performance indicators. Movements are assessed for accuracy across different positions and temperatures, cases are pressure tested for water resistance, and components like crowns and pushers are evaluated for strength and wear. Shock absorption is tested through impact simulations, and magnetic resistance is measured to ensure the watches remain stable when exposed to the kind of electromagnetic fields encountered in modern life.

Omega also conducts real-world testing through its involvement in scientific and exploratory missions. In 1989, it equipped Italian mountaineer Reinhold Messner with an Omega Seamaster for what would become the world's first crossing of the Antarctic by foot. Temperatures dropped to -40° Celsius and wind speed hit 145km/h, yet Messner made it – as did his watch. The journey took three months to complete, and throughout it he used his Seamaster for navigation. It was a landmark moment in field testing, reinforcing the brand's reputation for building watches that can withstand extremes.

Today, Omega continues to gather feedback from real-world use, whether through professional divers, environmental researchers or explorers operating in harsh and unpredictable environments. These practical trials complement the lab-based controls, ensuring that Omega watches are not only built to specification, but tested in the kinds of conditions they're designed to endure.

Materials

The materials a watch is made of can matter just as much as how it tells time. From deep-sea divers to dress watches, Omega has increasingly turned to advanced alloys, ceramics and composites. It has developed proprietary materials designed to address issues such as corrosion, wear and magnetic interference, as well as to make its designs stand out in a crowded market.

One example is Sedna Gold, its proprietary 18-karat rose gold alloy introduced in 2013. It combines gold, copper and palladium to create an alloy that has its own distinctive high-lustre shade and offers more protection against corrosion. It has also developed Canopus Gold, a bright-white 18-karat gold designed for durability and brilliance, and Moonshine Gold, an 18-karat yellow gold that has a paler hue than is standard.

For steel sports watches, Omega created O-Megasteel, a denser, more corrosion-resistant alloy that offers a slightly brighter finish than regular stainless steel, and added strength. It is used in its high-spec dive watches.

Omega has also turned its attention to ceramics. Bezels and cases in collections including Speedmaster and Seamaster are now frequently rendered in scratch-resistant ceramic, often paired with its proprietary Liquidmetal, a metallic alloy that fuses cleanly with ceramic to form bezel markings that won't wear down with use.

OPPOSITE: The Au750 mark in the dial identifies that it has been crafted in 18-karat gold.

ABOVE: Omega has developed its own alloys for gold bracelets, including Moonshine, Canopus and Sedna.

Museum

The Omega Museum in Biel/Bienne offers more than just a display of watches. It is a walk through the brand's history that takes in exploration, sporting excellence, cinema and design, packed with interesting exhibits, from Olymics timing tools to incredibly rare vintage and antique Omega watches.

Visitors can move through exhibits that highlight Omega's role in Olympic timekeeping, including a replica running track, its involvement in space missions, with cosmic displays that showcase real watches worn on the moon, and the audacious Alaska Project watches.

The watches worn in the James Bond films have their own dedicated area, placed in front of the original movie posters. There is also a naval uniform on display described as belonging to Commander Bond.

One of the most important and engaging exhibits in the museum is a chronological trail of timepieces, securely displayed in cabinets next to fascinating archival materials. It starts in 1848 and takes you through to 2023. Intriguing horological moments along the way include vintage advertisements, 19th century pocket watches and a minute repeater, war-time watches, and an Omega that once belonged to American president John F Kennedy, complete with a personalised engraving on the caseback. The museum is a must-see for any Omega fan.

OPPOSITE: These cases in the Omega Museum act as a timeline for the brand's history and are filled with artefacts.

ABOVE: The brand's space legacy is a key feature at the Omega Museum, and you can see actual watches that went into space.

Planet Omega

Omega's presence today is as visible on the red carpet as it is on sporting podiums. As the official timekeeper of the Olympic Games and a sponsor of global events like the America's Cup and PGA Tour, Omega continues to play an active role in international sport, and its growing list of celebrity ambassadors – from actors and athletes to musicians and models – has secured the brand its place in pop culture as much as in horological history. Whether launching limited editions with Hollywood stars, or timing split-second finishes at world-class competitions, Omega uses these partnerships to keep its watches firmly in the public eye.

LEFT: Clarence Maclin wore a Speedmaster Moonwatch in Sedna Gold on a black leather strap to the 30th Critics Choice Awards in 2024.

OPPOSITE: Ariana DeBose wearing a De Ville Trésor in Moonshine Gold to the 2024 Emmy Awards in Los Angeles.

Olympics and Paralympics

As the official timekeeper of the Olympic Games and Paralympic Games, Omega delivers the technology that ensures results are fair, accurate and indisputable. To do so, the brand uses innovations like sensor-equipped starting blocks, high-speed photo-finish cameras, laser and GPS tracking, and underwater touchpads in swimming. These systems also capture detailed performance data that can contribute to athlete analysis.

Omega's presence at the Games extends beyond timing the competition, with branded countdown clocks, on-screen graphics and themed watch releases tied to each Games. It also sets up a dedicated space at each Games, such as the Omega House in Soho for London 2012 and the Hôtel de Poulpry for Paris 2024. These club-style spaces draw athletes and other VIP guests of the brand. Guests at the Paris House included Nicole Kidman, Cindy Crawford, Daniel Craig, So-Hee Han and SDM.

The brand also supports a select group of elite Olympic athletes as ambassadors, including swimmer Michael Phelps, figure skater Nathan Chen, wheelchair fencer Bebe Vio, Paralympic triathlete Alexis Hanquinquant and triple jumper Yulimar Rojas.

OPPOSITE: A Moonshine Gold Seamaster with a commemorative caseback for the Milano Cortina 2026 Paralympic Winter Games.

ABOVE: The Seamaster Diver 300M created to celebrate the Paris 2024 Olympic Games.

Sailing

Omega's presence at the America's Cup puts it at the centre of sailing's most intense and innovative competition. As official timekeeper of the main event – along with the Youth and Women's America's Cup – the brand supports a sport where speed, strategy and technology collide. These races are measured in split seconds, and Omega's timing systems are built to capture every critical moment, from the start gun to the finish line.

It is also the official timekeeper of the SailGP catamaran race, one of the sport's most technologically advanced and globally watched events (in 2024 it attracted 293 million viewers), and is a long-time partner of America's Cup champions Emirates Team New Zealand.

Omega's sailing ambassadors include world champion Peter Burling, record-breaking British skipper Sir Ben Ainslie, and Olympic gold medallist Blair Tuke. Their involvement has inspired several sailing-themed timepieces, including limited editions of the Seamaster Diver 300M and Planet Ocean, designed with regatta-ready features and nods to the colours and identity of competitive sailing.

OPPOSITE: Sailors from America's Cup champions Emirates Team New Zealand.

RIGHT: Seamaster Planet Ocean 600M with turquoise detailing in homage to the logo colours of the Emirates Team New Zealand logo.

Swimming

In 1967, Omega developed touch-sensitive wall pads that allowed competitive swimmers to stop the clock themselves by hitting the wall, taking the subjectivity of a judge's gaze out of the equation. It has continued to innovate in underwater timing, introducing underwater lap counters and high-speed cameras. A notable demonstration of the accuracy of Omega's instruments came at the Beijing 2008 Olympics when Omega's equipment and cameras were used to confirm USA swimmer Michael Phelps' win in the 100m butterfly by just a hundredth of a second.

Omega's presence extends beyond the Olympic Games to events including the World Aquatics Championships and the TYR Pro Swim Series. It also has a number of ambassadors from the swimming world, including Phelps and the record-breaking French swimmer Léon Marchand. In 2017, Omega released the Seamaster Planet Ocean Michael Phelps Limited Edition. 280 pieces were made to reference Phelps' 28 Olympic medal count of 23 golds, three silvers and two bronze.

OPPOSITE: Athletes hold on to Omega starting blocks at a swimming event.

BELOW: Michael Phelps and Missy Franklin after receiving Omega High Point awards during the closing ceremony at the U.S. Olympic swimming trials in 2012.

Bobsleigh

Omega's connection to bobsleigh events dates back to the 1930s, when it first began timing winter sports at the Olympic Games. Today, that legacy continues through Omega's partnership with the Olympics, and also the International Bobsleigh and Skeleton Federation (IBSF), which it partnered with in 2002 to time all IBSF events.

Omega times bobsleigh events using a combination of photoelectric sensors and its advanced Omega Measurement Unit, a compact device fitted to the sled that records real-time data such as speed, acceleration, and G-forces throughout the run. This captures the full dynamics of each descent, to be shared with the teams and TV viewers in real time.

In 2001, Omega supported the launch of a new winter sport, monobob. This bobsleigh-adjacent sport features a single athlete piloting a sled from start to finish. The timing demands are the same, with the sled exceeding speeds of 120 km/h on winding ice tracks with rapid transitions.

OPPOSITE: Singer-songwriter Cian Ducrot takes part in a celebrity bobsleigh event.

LEFT: Actress Wallis Day poses with an Omega-branded bobsleigh in St. Moritz.

Golf

Omega has established a strong presence in professional golf as the official timekeeper of the Omega European Masters since 2001. The event is one of the longest-running tournaments in Europe, founded in 1923 and held at the Crans-sur-Sierre golf club in Valais, Switzerland, each September.

It is also a partner of multiple Professional Golfers' Association (PGA) and Ladies Professional Golf Association (LPGA) events. Omega has been keen to support women's golf, working with players including Michelle Wie West, Danielle Kang and Charley Hull to bring more attention to the sport.

On the course, Omega's timekeeping is visible at key holes and integrated into event branding, while off the course, the brand supports the sport through limited editions and ambassador partnerships. Golfers like Rory McIlroy, who became an ambassador in 2013, have helped connect Omega to the world of elite competition by wearing its watches. McIlroy's go-to choice is the Seamaster Aqua Terra Ultra Light, designed with lightweight titanium and a push-in crown to minimise wrist interference while playing.

OPPOSITE: Spain's Sergio García plays at the Omega Masters.

TOP RIGHT: Swiss golfer and Omega ambassador Morgane Métraux.

RIGHT: South Korean actor and Omega ambassador Hyun Bin poses at a golf event.

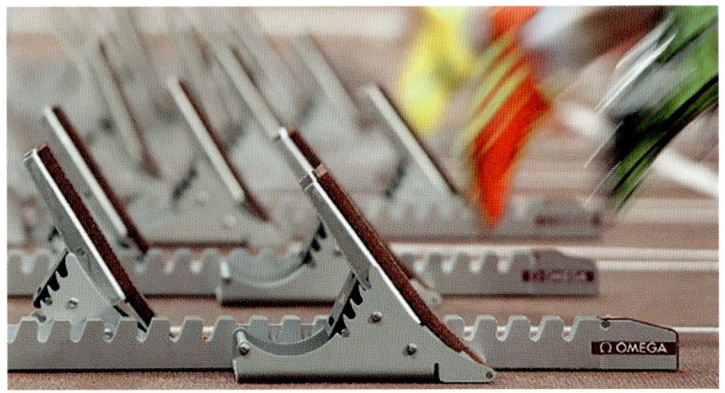

Athletics

Omega provides the timing systems used at many of the world's leading athletics events including the Olympic Games, World Athletics Championships and the Wanda Diamond League, a global series of top-tier track and field meetings held across four continents. From sprinting and hurdles to jumps and throws, Omega's role includes monitoring reaction times, detecting false starts and delivering high-speed photo finishes.

The brand's Scan'O'Vision camera, which captures up to 40,000 digital images per second, is a fixture at these events, helping officials determine outcomes in races where finishes are too close to judge by eye. At the 2019 World Athletics Championships in Doha, Omega introduced real-time heat mapping and athlete tracking technology, offering broadcasters new insights into pacing, positioning, and how races unfolded across the track.

As with all the sports it supports, Omega has enlisted a team of ambassadors from athletics, including Noah Lyles, Mondo Duplantis and Shelly-Ann Fraser-Pryce.

OPPOSITE: Omega has developed timed starting blocks for running races.

ABOVE: American track and field sprinter Noah Lyles is one of Omega's athletics ambassadors.

Omega on Film

Omega has become a familiar sight both on screen and on the red carpet, with its watches appearing in major films, and on the wrists of some of cinema's most recognisable names. Nowhere is this relationship more established than in the James Bond franchise. Omega has been Bond's watch of choice for the past nine films, first worn by Pierce Brosnan in 1995's *Golden Eye* through to Daniel Craig's *No Time to Die* performance in 2021.

Omega watches have also appeared in films where precision timekeeping plays a central role in the story. In *Apollo 13* and *First Man*, the Speedmaster was featured in recognition of its real-life connection to NASA's space programme, while in *Ad Astra*, it became a symbol of scientific reliability in a futuristic setting.

During the filming of *First Man*, Omega worked closely with the production team to ensure historical accuracy. The watches used were period-correct recreations of the Speedmaster worn on the real Apollo 11 mission.

OPPOSITE: Colman Domingo wore a Sedna Gold De Ville Trésor with a burgundy dial and strap to the 30th Critics Choice Awards in 2024.

ABOVE: A display of Bond movie watches and memorabilia at the Omega Museum in Biel/Bienne.

Off screen, the brand maintains close ties with the film industry through its roster of ambassadors. Nicole Kidman, Eddie Redmayne and George Clooney (whose first watch was an Omega, long before he signed a contract with the brand) are among those who represent it, wearing its watches to premieres, festivals, and award shows. Omega regularly appears at the Venice International Film Festival, using the event as a platform to highlight its ongoing connection to cinema. As a festival sponsor, the brand is often seen on the red carpet, worn by its ambassadors and guests. At the 81st edition in 2024, Daniel Craig, promoting his film *Queer*, wore two different Omega watches in a single day – a Seamaster 300 with a nato strap and a Seamaster Aqua Terra 150M.

Elsewhere, you will spot Omega watches on red carpets from London to Los Angeles, as its ambassadors – and timepieces – regularly attend major film events around the world, including the Oscars, Golden Globes, BAFTAs, SAG Awards, and the Cannes Film Festival.

OPPOSITE: Nicole Kidman wore an Art Nouveau Omega platinum timepiece from 1920, set with 24 diamonds, to the 82nd Golden Globes in 2025.

ABOVE: Daniel Craig wore a Seamaster Aqua Terra 150M with a black dial to the premier of *Queer* during the Venice Film Festival in 2024.

The Art of Collecting

Collectors are drawn to Omega watches for their design, technical quality and cultural significance. From early pocket watches to space-flown Speedmasters and rare limited editions, each piece offers a glimpse into the brand's evolving identity. The world of Omega collecting spans iconic models and hidden gems that have gained status through innovation, provenance or sheer rarity. A military-issued Seamaster, a 1970s De Ville with experimental styling, or a Speedmaster worn during a key moment in history all offer something unique to the collector. For many, collecting Omega is about discovery – a way to connect with watchmaking history, one reference at a time.

ABOVE: The Omega Semaster Aqua Terra 150M ref. 231.10.42.21.03.003.

OPPOSITE: The bioceramic MoonSwatch watches have become a hugely popular collector's item.

Vintage Omega

What draws collectors to vintage Omega is often less about the brand name and more about the details that turn a watch into a story. The right font, a stepped dial, a set of lyre lugs untouched by overzealous polishing – these are the things that make collectors lean in. A pie-pan Constellation with crisp bevels and an original bracelet isn't just elegant, it is symbolic of a moment in mid-century watchmaking when Omega was pushing to outpace its rivals in both style and chronometric accuracy. A Seamaster 300 with military engravings tells its own story; its value shaped not just by its rarity, but by the life it has lived.

The appeal of vintage Omega lies in this sense of discovery. A reference might be overlooked for years, then suddenly gain cult status as collectors start to appreciate a subtle design quirk or rediscover a connection to a historical event. One such example is the Omega Flightmaster, a bold, aviator-inspired GMT chronograph launched in 1969 and discontinued in 1977. While

its original run was short, its unusual design and association with the now-romanticised era of supersonic travel have made collectors take a fresh look, and today it is a sought-after timepiece on the secondary market.

What makes a collector tick – provenance, rarity, a quirky flaw – varies, but certain Omega watches stand out as true collectors' items. These include the Speedmaster Snoopy editions (particularly the 2003 Silver Snoopy and 2015 white-dial version), the Seamaster Diver 300M 007 Edition as worn by Daniel Craig in *No Time To Die*, and the Speedmaster Dark Side of the Moon watches.

OPPOSITE: A vintage CK2444 military wristwatch produced specifically for the British Ministry of Defence during World War II.

BELOW: An Omega CK2292, which was used by World War II navigators in the British Royal Air Force.

Speedy Tuesdays

What started as a simple social media post became one of the most influential online movements in modern watch collecting. In 2012, the team behind Fratello Watches – a Dutch-based online magazine and one of the first dedicated watch blogs – posted a photo of a

Speedmaster with the hashtag #SpeedyTuesday. The idea caught on quickly. Within weeks, collectors around the world were posting their own Speedmaster shots each Tuesday, sharing stories, reference numbers and personal connections to the watch. What followed was the birth of a digital community built entirely around one model, united by a shared obsession with design, history and detail.

Omega recognised the power of the movement. In 2017, it released the first official Speedy Tuesday edition – a limited-run Speedmaster with a reverse panda dial, vintage-style logo, and radial subdials. It sold out in a matter of hours. A second model followed in 2018, inspired by the Ultraman Speedmaster of the 1970s, complete with an orange chrono hand and playful nods to its sci-fi roots. Both releases were sold exclusively online and marketed directly to the Speedy Tuesday audience.

Beyond the watches themselves, Speedy Tuesday has evolved into a global platform. Omega now hosts regular Speedy Tuesday events, bringing collectors together in cities around the world. What began as a fan-led initiative has become part of the brand's own story, a rare example of collectors and company shaping a legacy together.

OPPOSITE: This 2017 Speedmaster Speedy Tuesday was based on the 1978 Alaska Project II.

Rare Omegas

Some Omega watches are rare by intention – others by accident. Either way, the appeal lies in their scarcity, technical interest and ability to mark turning points in the brand's story. One of the most coveted is the Speedmaster CK2915, the first-ever Speedmaster, launched in 1957. With its broad arrow hands, steel bezel and clean, functional dial, it set the blueprint for one of the most recognisable chronographs in history, but only for a short time. Produced for just two years, surviving examples now rank among Omega's most desirable vintage pieces.

Even fewer were made of the Alaska Project prototypes. Built for NASA in the late 1960s and early 1970s, these experimental Speedmasters were designed to withstand extreme conditions in space. Featuring oversized red-anodised aluminium cases and heavily modified internals, they never made it to public sale, and remain almost mythical among collectors.

OPPOSITE: An Omega Megaquartz 2400 marine chronometer.

BELOW: A 1957 CK2915-1, the very first Speedmaster (below), next to a modern 18-karat Canopus gold Speedmaster Calibre 321 inspired by it.

Other rarities appeared in more unexpected forms. The Marine Chronometer of 1974 was the world's first wristwatch certified as a marine chronometer, with only 1,000 pieces produced. The Chrono-Quartz Albatross, launched at the 1976 Montreal Olympics, was another technical outlier as the world's first analogue-digital chronograph, and now trades among collectors for thousands.

In the modern era, the Seamaster 300 Spectre Limited Edition, released in 2015 for the James Bond film of the same name, proved how cinematic connection and small design tweaks – it has a lollipop seconds hand and 12-hour bezel – could make a watch instantly collectible.

Omega's rarest watches reflect the brand's ability to surprise, and the collector's instinct to chase what's hard to find. And the MoonSwatch, a playful, affordable collaboration between Omega and Swatch that first launched in 2022, proved that a watch doesn't need a high price

tag or an incredibly limited run to become instantly collectible. These watches, inspired by the Speedmaster Moonwatch and made in colourful bioceramic, have led to huge crowds queuing outside Swatch boutiques for a chance to buy one.

OPPOSITE LEFT: An Omega Seamaster 300 Spectre edition shot in an Aston Martin Vanquish Volante for *T3* magazine in 2015.

OPPOSITE RIGHT: A special edition James Bond Seamaster Aqua Terra in a commemorative *No Time to Die* box.

ABOVE: In 2024, 11 suitcases containing all of the 11 Omega x Swatch Mission to Moonshine Gold watches were auctioned through Sotheby's, with the top lot being the Beijing-themed box that sold for CHF60,960.

Omegas at Auction

In the world of watch auctions, Omega has achieved remarkable milestones, with certain timepieces fetching record-breaking prices due to their historical significance and rarity.

In 2018, Elvis Presley's Omega wristwatch, an 18-karat white gold timepiece adorned with 44 brilliant-cut diamonds, was sold for a world record price of CHF1.5 million at Phillips. This watch, presented to Elvis by RCA Records in 1961 to commemorate 75 million records sold, is considered one of the most historically significant Elvis Presley-owned watches to ever appear on the market.

Another notable sale occurred in 2017 when an Omega Stainless Steel Tourbillon 301 was auctioned by Phillips for approximately CHF1.42 million. This timepiece, coveted for its technical innovation, was the most expensive Omega timepiece sold at auction at that time.

Additionally, in 2024, the one-millionth MoonSwatch, a special edition of the affordable bioceramic version of Omega's Speedmaster, was auctioned for nearly $80,000 at a fundraising auction held by Christie's to support the European Leukodystrophy Association. This particular model, a blue Mission to Neptune design with Moonshine gold-coated seconds hand and a commemorative '1,000,000' engraving, had been expected to fetch $1,000 but the final hammer price was nearly 290 times its original retail price of $270.

These exceptional sales underscore the enduring appeal and collectability of Omega watches, and the passion of collectors worldwide

OPPOSITE: This prototype, one of eight Omega Seamaster 300 wristwatches, worn by Daniel Craig as James Bond, sold at Christie's for £92,500 in 2016.

ABOVE: A Christie's employee shows an 18-karat gold Moonwatch Apollo IX circa 1969, ref No 145, sold for CHF 22,500 in 2015.

Positive Impact

Omega's role extends beyond precision timekeeping. The brand has aligned itself with projects that seek to make a difference, from safeguarding the oceans to supporting humanitarian initiatives and tackling the growing issue of space debris. These efforts reflect a broader ambition: to use Omega's visibility not just to promote watches, but to support meaningful change. Through long-term partnerships, funding and awareness campaigns, Omega is using its platform to contribute to causes that matter, both on Earth and beyond.

ABOVE: The Omega factory in Biel-Bienne was built as an eco-friendly building by architect Shigeru Ban.

OPPOSITE: The factory is fitted with 1,770 square meters of photovoltaic panels, generating around 212.3 MWh of electricity each year,

Sustainability At Sea

Omega's connection to the ocean goes beyond the depths reached by its dive watches. The brand actively supports marine conservation through partnerships that combine science, community and advocacy. One such example is its support for the coastal village of Bahoi in North Sulawesi, Indonesia, where local communities are being empowered to manage Marine Protected Areas – designated areas in the ocean that are established to protect habitats, species and ecosystems essential for the health and functioning of marine environments. The project aims to protect coral reefs – a critical economic and ecological asset – while supporting eco-tourism and education around sustainable fishing practices.

In partnership with Nekton, a not-for-profit research foundation, Omega has also helped fund deep-sea scientific missions, including the 2020 First Descent expedition in the Seychelles. Using submersibles and advanced data collection tools, researchers gathered vital information about unexplored areas of the seabed and the effects of climate change on fragile marine ecosystems.

Omega's support of Live Ocean, a marine conservation charity founded by Olympic sailors Peter Burling and Blair Tuke, adds another layer to its sea-focused efforts. The initiative is dedicated to protecting and restoring ocean health, with an emphasis on public engagement and scientific research in New Zealand and beyond. Through Live Ocean, Omega backs work that addresses biodiversity loss, marine pollution and ocean warming – some of the most pressing environmental issues of our time.

OPPOSITE: The Omega Seamaster Diver 300M Co-Axial Master Chronometer Nekton Edition.

ABOVE: A Nekton submarine with Omega branding.

GoodPlanet Foundation

Omega's partnership with the GoodPlanet Foundation reflects a shared commitment to environmental education and marine conservation. Together, they have supported impactful projects and storytelling initiatives that raise awareness of ecological challenges.

One of the most high-profile collaborations was the 2012 documentary Planet Ocean, directed by Yann Arthus-Bertrand and Michael Pitiot, which explored the beauty and fragility of marine life and was screened at the United Nations.

Omega and GoodPlanet have also backed community-led projects such as a mangrove restoration programme on Indonesia's Tanakeke Island, and a large-scale seagrass conservation initiative in Madagascar's Ranobe Bay. These efforts aim to restore vital ecosystems, protect biodiversity and support food security for local populations who depend on the ocean for survival.

OPPOSITE: Actor Josh Duhamel and director Yann Arthus-Bertrand at the launch of Planet Ocean in Hollywood in 2013.

BELOW: A screening of the Planet Ocean documentary.

Space Debris

Increasing space exploration has brought with it a less visible consequence: a growing field of debris orbiting the Earth. The European Space Agency (ESA) estimates that there are more than 1 million objects – pieces of inactive satellites, spent rocket parts, collision fragments – circling the planet, threatening active spacecraft and complicating future missions. Managing this waste has become one of the most pressing challenges in the space industry.

Omega, long connected to spaceflight through the Speedmaster, has turned its attention to the issue of orbital debris. The brand has partnered with scientists and agencies in developing tools to track and mitigate the risk posed by space junk. This includes support for awareness initiatives, as well as collaboration with experts designing systems to monitor and potentially clear debris from low-Earth orbit.

In 2022, Omega worked with Swiss astronaut Claude Nicollier and a network of European researchers exploring solutions for sustainable space operations. Among them were projects to improve satellite traffic management and reduce the chances of future collisions.

It has also partnered with Privateer (led by Apple co-founder Steve Wozniak, Ripcord CEO and founder Alex Fielding and astrodynamicist and space environmentalist Dr. Moriba Jah), which is working to map the space junk orbiting our planet. Every visual Privateer captures is time stamped with an Omega watch showing the time. Its work so far suggests the problem might be even bigger than the ESA figures would suggest, with Privateer's calculations putting the number of individual space debris closer to 100 million.

OPPOSITE: L-R: Omega president and CEO Raynald Aeschlimann, former astronaut Professor Claude Nicollier, and ClearSpace CEO Luc Piguet.

ABOVE: ClearSpace debris clean up in action as it removes space junk from the Earth's orbit.

Orbis

Omega's partnership with Orbis International highlights the brand's ongoing support for global health initiatives. Orbis is a non-profit organisation working to prevent avoidable blindness in under-served communities. Its Flying Eye Hospital – a fully equipped teaching facility inside an aircraft – delivers specialist care and trains local medical teams in regions with limited access to eye health services.

ABOVE: Approximately 500,000 children go blind each year, with a high number of the cases being prevantable.

Through this partnership, Omega contributes to fundraising, medical outreach and awareness-building efforts. The brand's support helps enable surgeries, expand training programmes and bring long-term benefits to communities that might otherwise go without care.

To mark its involvement, Omega has created De Ville Trésor Orbis editions featuring subtle design details linked to the charity, including a teddy bear motif on the caseback to reference the toys given to young patients.

ABOVE: Omega donates cuddly teddy bears, called Seymour, to help provide comfort and support to children recovering from eye surgery.

An Eco Build

When architect Shigeru Ban received the commission to design Omega's main manufacturing facility in Biel/Bienne, which opened in 2017, he was given a clear directive: to ensure that it was a sustainable build.

The structure utilises timber and concrete, with approximately 4,600 cubic meters of Swiss spruce employed in its construction. Remarkably, the entire volume of wood used in the building can be replenished by Switzerland's abundant forests in just a few hours, according to official figures, demonstrating just how sustainable a choice the locally sourced spruce is.

Energy efficiency at the manufacturer is achieved through a combination of geothermal systems and solar technology. Several underground wells provide groundwater for heating and cooling, reducing reliance on fossil fuels. Additionally, the building is fitted with 1,770 square meters of photovoltaic panels, generating around

212.3 MWh of electricity annually, the equivalent of powering 61 Swiss households.

The building's design also incorporates natural ventilation, high-performance insulation and rainwater harvesting systems, further minimising its environmental footprint. Inside, the use of natural materials and ample daylight creates a comfortable working environment, aligning with Omega's commitment to employee wellbeing.

By integrating these eco-conscious features, Omega's Biel/Bienne facility stands as a testament to the brand's dedication to reducing environmental impact while maintaining the precision and quality synonymous with Swiss watchmaking.

OPPOSITE: The new Omega headquarters opened in Biel/Bienne in 2017.

ABOVE: Local Swiss spruce has been used for the construction of the building.

Enduring Legacy

Omega stands as one of the most influential names in Swiss watchmaking, blending heritage with innovation to maintain its global prominence. Each year it produces around 700,000 watches, with sales figures that stretch into the billions. A LuxeConsult and Morgan Stanley report released in 2025 estimated that Omega, as a single brand, represented 7% of the Swiss watch market, ranking it among the top three brands worldwide behind Rolex and Cartier.

The brand's success is bolstered by its iconic models, such as the Speedmaster and Seamaster, which continue to captivate both seasoned collectors and new enthusiasts. Collaborations like the MoonSwatch have also introduced Omega to a younger demographic, demonstrating its ability to innovate while honouring its legacy.

Omega's role as the official timekeeper for the Olympic Games and its association with cultural icons like James Bond further cement its status in both sports and popular culture. These partnerships not only enhance brand visibility but also underscore Omega's commitment to precision and excellence. And in the digital realm, Omega has effectively leveraged celebrity endorsements and social media to engage with a global audience, ranking among the top watch brands in digital performance.

Omega's enduring legacy is a testament to its ability to evolve with the times while staying true to its core values of quality, innovation, and style. As the brand continues to navigate the future, it remains a symbol of excellence in watchmaking, and one of the most coveted, collectible watch brands in the world.

OPPOSITE AND OVERLEAF: The interior of Omega's K11 Musea Hong Kong boutique.

ABOVE: K11 Musea is a shopping area in Hong Kong that is home to many luxury brands, including Omega.

Image Credits

(t) = top, (b) = bottom, (c) = centre, (l) = left, (r) = right

Page 6 Omega; 7 Omega; 8 Omega; 9 Omega; 10 Omega; 11 Omega; 12 Omega; 13 Bill Waterson/Alamy; 14 Omega; 15 Kumar Sriskandan/Alamy; 16 Kumar Sriskandan/Alamy; 18 Omega; 19 Everett Collection/Shutterstock; 20 Omega; 21 Omega; 22 Omega; 23 Omega; 24-25 Omega; 26 Omega; 27 Tubray Media/Alamy; 28 Associated Press/Alamy; 29 Associated Press/Alamy; 30 Omega; 31 Omega; 32 Omega; 33 Omega; 35 Omega; 36 Omega; 37 Omega; 38 Omega; 39 Omega; 40 Omega; 41 Omega; 42 Kumar Sriskandan/Alamy; 43 Omega; 44 David Wei/Alamy; 45 OnTheRoad/Alamy; 46 Mike Marsland/Getty; 47 Omega; 48 PA Images/Alamy; 49 Omega; 50 Omega; 51 Omega; 52 TOSHIFUMI KITAMURA/Getty; 53 adsR/Alamy; 54 Omega; 55 Smith Archive/Alamy; 56 Omega; 57 Omega; 59 Omega; 60 Omega; 61 Omega; 62 Omega; 63 Omega; 64 Omega; 65 Colin McPherson/Alamy; 67 TOSHIFUMI KITAMURA/Getty; 68 Omega; 69 Omega; 70 Omega; 71 Omega; 72 Omega; 73 Omega; 75 Grzegorz Czapski;

76 Omega; 77 Omega; 78 Omega; 79 Omega; 80 Omega; 81 Omega; 82 Omega; 83 Omega; 84 Omega; 85 Omega; 86 Omega; 87 Omega; 88 Omega; 89 Omega; 90 Omega; 91 Omega; 92 Omega; 93 Omega; 94 Omega; 95 Omega; 96-97 Omega; 98 Omega; 99 Omega; 100 Omega; 101 Omega; 102 Omega; 103 Omega; 104 Omega; 105 Omega; 106 Omega; 108 Tubray Media/Alamy; 109 Tubray Media/Alamy; 110 Omega; 111 Omega; 112 Michael Kovac/Getty; 113 Omega; 114 Omega; 115 Omega; 116 Omega; 117 Omega; 118 Sergio Azenha/Alamy; 119 Associated Press/Alamy; 120 Omega; 121 Omega; 122 Omega; 123 Omega; 124 Omega; 125 Omega; 126 Omega; 127 Omega; 128 Amy Sussman/Getty; 129 Omega; 130 Omega; 131 Omega; 132 Omega; 133 Omega; 134-135 Omega; 136 Science & Society Picture Library/Getty; 137 Omega; 138 (l) Future Publishing/Getty; 138 (r) Omega; 139 Omega; 140 PA Images/Alamy; 141 Associated Press/Alamy; 142 Omega; 143 Omega; 144 Omega; 145 Omega; 146 Angela Weiss/Getty; 147 Dimitrios Kambouris/Getty; 148 Omega; 149 Omega; 150 Omega; 151 Omega; 152 Omega; 153 Omega; 154 Omega; 155 Omega; 156-157 Omega.

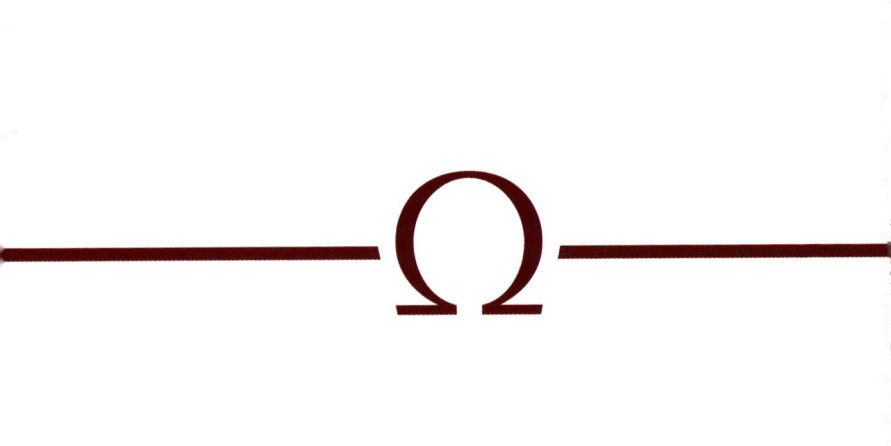